Cambridge Elements ≡

Elements in Psycholinguistics
edited by
Paul Warren
Victoria University of Wellington

T0287019

DYNAMIC APPROACHES TO PHONOLOGICAL PROCESSING

Hunter Hatfield
University of Otago

CAMBRIDGE
UNIVERSITY PRESS

Shaftesbury Road, Cambridge CB2 8EA, United Kingdom

One Liberty Plaza, 20th Floor, New York, NY 10006, USA

477 Williamstown Road, Port Melbourne, VIC 3207, Australia

314–321, 3rd Floor, Plot 3, Splendor Forum, Jasola District Centre,
New Delhi – 110025, India

103 Penang Road, #05–06/07, Visioncrest Commercial, Singapore 238467

Cambridge University Press is part of Cambridge University Press & Assessment,
a department of the University of Cambridge.

We share the University's mission to contribute to society through the pursuit of
education, learning and research at the highest international levels of excellence.

www.cambridge.org
Information on this title: www.cambridge.org/9781009258685

DOI: 10.1017/9781009258661

First published 2023

A catalogue record for this publication is available from the British Library.

ISBN 978-1-009-25868-5 Paperback
ISSN 2753-9768 (online)
ISSN 2753-975X (print)

Dynamic Approaches to Phonological Processing

Elements in Psycholinguistics

DOI: 10.1017/9781009258661
First published online: April 2023

Hunter Hatfield
University of Otago

Author for correspondence: Hunter Hatfield, hunter.hatfield@otago.ac.nz

Abstract: Natural language occurs in time. Events happen earlier, later, or simultaneously with other events; however, this temporal dimension is often downplayed or overlooked. This Element introduces readers with a background in structural linguistics to dynamic approaches to phonological processing. It covers models of serial order, speech production, and speech perception, with special attention to how they can enhance one another. It then asks whether dynamic approaches have the potential to change how we think of phonological structure. Key ideas discussed include phonemes and auditory targets, control mechanisms creating structure, and the shape of phonological representations in a dynamic context. The Element should function as a bridge for those with linguistic questions who want to learn answers derived from the study of speech as a dynamic system.

Keywords: psycholinguistics, speech production, speech perception, dynamic systems, phonology

ISBNs: 9781009258685 (PB), 9781009258661 (OC)
ISSNs: 2753-9768 (online), 2753-975X (print)

Contents

1 Introduction   1

2 Serial Order   4

3 Speech Production   14

4 Speech Perception   27

5 Dynamic Intention Selection and Coordination   40

6 Gathering Key Ideas   51

7 Approaching a Dynamic Model of Speech
  and Phonology   56

8 Conclusion   61

  References   66

1 Introduction

1.1 Language in Space and Time

In 1916, Ferdinand de Saussure's *Course in General Linguistics* launched structural linguistics and structuralism in social science. A century later, the introduction to linguistics at my own university was titled *Linguistics and Its Structure*. When we think of structures literally, we think of physical things in space, structures like buildings or how bones of an animal fit together. For most of its history, linguistic theory has been expressed via a metaphor of objects arranged in space. We see this repeatedly in many sub-fields of linguistics.

- When writing phonological rules, we say things like one phone is to the <u>left</u> of, the <u>right</u> of, or <u>between</u> other phones.
- An infix is a morpheme <u>inside</u> another morpheme.
- Syllables or phrase structure are commonly expressed via trees where one unit is <u>above</u>, <u>below</u>, or <u>beside</u> another unit.
- Phonology can be said to have <u>layers</u>.
- A language's syntax can be <u>left</u>- or <u>right</u>-branching.
- Within psycholinguistics, we talk about <u>top-down</u> and <u>bottom-up</u> processing.

This predominant use of a spatial metaphor for language becomes surprising when reflecting on natural language, such as a conversation, monologue, or internal thought. Spoken and signed language is ephemeral with little realisation in physical space at all. The physical vibration in space of air molecules dissipates back into the environment incredibly quickly. Fluctuations in the electromagnetic field of our brain or the bodily movement of speech gestures vanish just as fast. While a speaker's tongue certainly occupies physical space, its movement left and right in the mouth does not translate to what linguists mean when phonemes are left or right of each other. Rather than left or right, speech sounds occur *earlier* or *later* than one another.

In short, while linguistic theory is often expressed in terms of a spatial dimension (*in, out, above, below, left, right*), natural language has a strong temporal dimension.

Temporal and spatial dimensions are not mutually exclusive, of course. Language occurs in both. The point here is simply that the temporal dimension of speech is far less researched and considered than a spatial one. This default to spatial language might be because the dominant mode of communicating linguistic theory to a broad audience has been through journals and textbooks, wherein temporally transient language is rendered into semi-permanent spatial configurations via writing. On the page, a symbol indicating a phoneme is indeed to the left of or right of another. On the page with a linguistic tree structure, a syntactic level is above a morphological one, which is above a phonological one. This is an artefact of writing, of course. When we write using a language's orthography or IPA, a letter (sound) may be to the left of another, but when we speak, the sound is in fact earlier than another. Sounds written on the right are after in time (in left–right orthographies like English). In a spatial tree structure, when X is a node immediately above Y and joined to it, X *contains* Y. In time, Y is inside X when X starts before and ends after Y.

The question for this Element will be: does it matter? Does it matter that something is before something else, rather than to the left/right of it? Or are those equivalent? Does the temporal structure of language affect how we theorise about language? The fact that writing systems can proceed from left to right or right to left or top to bottom, while always being spoken the same way, suggests language is ambivalent about its spatial representation.

This Element narrows the question further. Rather than ask our questions of all of linguistic theory, it will focus only on what is most frequently expressed as 'language at the word level and <u>below</u>'. Expressed in temporal terms, we will focus on processes that happen over about one second of speech, enough for five syllables. In other words, we will look at speech production and perception of words, as well as their phonological patterning. Actions that take longer, such as putting morphemes into phrases, their meaning, their use, and conversation will all be reserved for later work.

The term *dynamic* will be used here in the general sense of 'changing over time', rather than a single approach to the dynamics of language (see also van Geert 1991, 2003). We will sometimes use dynamic systems theory, but this Element works off the principle that, if language changes states over time, it is a dynamic approach to language. The three main aspects of time we will use are:

1. Events can occur earlier, later, or simultaneously with other events. This aspect focuses on temporal sequencing or, using the term most common in psychology, **serial order**.
2. Events have a certain **duration**. They last for a certain amount of time.
3. Events or entities can change over time. This is the study of **dynamics**.

These can be rephrased into a non-exhaustive set of questions that are profitable to ask.

1. How do we produce, perceive, and remember sequences of speech in time?
2. How do we control, produce, and perceive speech durations in time?
3. What are the dynamics of speech?

This Element serves at least two purposes. The first is as a primer to temporal/ dynamic approaches to language. The second is to stop and think about language itself. We want to discover whether asking questions about **time** in language changes how we think of the **structures** of language. In other words, is temporal linguistics an implementation detail of linguistic structure, or does temporal linguistics in fact change structural linguistics itself?

1.2 Who Is This Element For?

The goal of this Element is to introduce people familiar with classic structural linguistics to dynamic approaches to language. By classic structural linguistics, I mean concepts familiar from a year or two of linguistics in most curricula. Sentences are made up of phrases, phrases of words, and words of morphemes. Phonologically, word-sized units contain syllables and syllables contain phonemes. Phonemes in turn can be expressed as contextually dependent allophones, often in a form like:

/phoneme/ ➔ [allophone] / In a particular phonetic environment.

Following such a pattern, the process of vowel nasalisation for /o/ could be written as:

/o/ ➔ [õ] / ____ [nasal]

The reader may know of optimality theory (OT) and how it is a system of constraints that choose an optimal output. This Element will compare its ideas against OT but never engage in doing OT. The following list states what knowledge this Element assumes:

- Introductory articulatory phonetics. You should be comfortable with terms from the IPA like alveolar, palatal, velar, plosives, fricatives, and so on. You will be able to recall their articulatory meanings. For instance, an alveolar involves a tongue tip movement to the alveolar ridge. Similarly, an [s] requires the tongue tip be close but not touch the ridge, while a [t] will have full closure.
- Introductory acoustic phonetics. Familiar terms here would include amplitude, spectrograph, formants, bursts, periodicity, and so on. You will not need to read spectrograms, calculate a Nyquist frequency, or utilise spectral analysis techniques, such as FFT or LPC, but we will utilise spectral analysis conceptually.
- Concepts like phonemes, allophones, distinctive features, syllables, and stress. We will spend much of the Element questioning these very concepts, but these are the starting point. We will also look at metrical phonology wherein languages can assign stress based upon weight, count morae or syllables, and move directionally left to right or right to left (but what does left to right mean if we shift from a spatial metaphor for language to a temporal one?).

- Morphosyntax. This text will not delve into morphosyntax. It only assumes concepts such as morphemes, being the smallest piece of language with meaning, and that morphemes can build words and phrases.

Finally, because this Element is part of the Psycholinguistics series from Cambridge University Press, it assumes you are familiar with common questions of psycholinguistics and some of the techniques. You would know what speech perception, speech production, and word recognition are, as well as generally how these questions are studied. However, I do not expect the reader to have Levelt's (1993) model of speech production in mind, be able to recall the details of TRACE (McClelland & Elman, 1986), and so on.

This Element's assumptions about your knowledge are based on the purposes of the text. One reason dynamic approaches have not received as much attention as they warrant is they can be challenging for a linguist of typical training. Just as it would be difficult to pick up an article deriving prosodic patterns via OT when you have not studied structural linguistics, research on dynamic systems approaches can challenge linguists. It can be easy to get lost in the technical terminology of attractors, limit cycles, evolving systems, differential equations, and more. *Dynamic Approaches to Phonological Processing*[1] hopes to build a bridge from structural linguistics to this dynamic literature. To accomplish this:

- This Element simplifies models. Sub-components are sometimes left out or technical details are passed over. As one example, Turk and Shattuck-Hufnagel's (2020) book *Speech Timing: Implications for Theories of Phonology, Phonetics, and Speech Motor Control* covers its ideas over 300 pages. We will cover their theory in fewer than 5 pages. Every theory presented here is in fact richer, more substantiated, and precise than this work has space for. I hope this Element can prepare the reader to approach the original work for full engagement.
- The Element offers a select set of dynamic models and does not attempt a comprehensive look as a review article might. Covering such breadth would sacrifice the space for introducing concepts at the right introductory level or going deep enough into some to highlight their potential value.

2 Serial Order

Any complete model of language will eventually need to specify how things are put into and kept in the right order. In a spoken conversation (as opposed to

---

[1] Phonetic transcriptions by default will be in New Zealand English, based on Bauer and colleagues' (2007) analysis. Exceptions include using transcriptions from research and a couple of points where alternate transcription allows for easier explication.

written text), order requires saying some items before or after other items, which means taking certain actions at certain times. Therefore, serial order is inherently about controlling when to do something. The items to order might be phrases, words, morphemes, syllables, phones, all the way to gestures of the hands or vocal tract. If we are listening, we also need to process the units of language as they arrive in some order as well. Was this acoustic burst, phone, word, phrase, or clause first or second? Even if incoming material is processed immediately, any ability to reflect on what was previously said requires knowing what 'previous' is.

The question of serial order is hiding in every IPA transcription or statement that a certain series of phonemes is the phonemic representation of a word. As Kazanina, Bowers, and Idsardi (2018) state,

> A traditional answer from linguistic theory . . . is that words are represented in long-term memory as sequences of phonemes, that is, abstract and discrete symbolic units of a size of an individual speech segment, such as a consonants or vowel (yet not identical to them). *A phonological form of a word is an ordered sequence* of phonemes, for example, the sequence of phonemes /k/ – /æ/ – /t/ (more succinctly, /kæt/) refers to a meowing domesticated feline animal or /dʌk/ to a quacking avian. (561; emphasis added)

In short, every single word with a phonological representation requires learning, maintaining, and producing a serial order, a sequence of actions in time. The phonological form of a word is, therefore, two things: a set of phonemes and an order of those phonemes. Phonemes are categorical units capable of building lexical contrasts, but a set of phonemes is not sufficient to represent a lexical item: the phonemes' order must also be specified and remembered. We would not understand a lexical representation without understanding serial order. How one maintains serial order for phonemic representations is not commonly addressed in linguistics textbooks – but we will do so now.

Two seminal works from the 1950s have guided the study of serial order and serial recall. One is Lashley's (1951) *The Problem of Serial Order in Behavior*, which documented how turning hierarchical mental structures into serial actions was a fundamental question across a range of behaviours. The second seminal work is Miller's (1956) 'The magical number seven, plus or minus two: Some limits on our capacity for processing information'. Miller's article claimed humans can hold about seven items in what came to be called working memory, based primarily upon research in the serial recall experimental task. In such an experiment, a participant is presented with a list of items, usually short words, and must repeat them in order. For example, the participant hears *nine, four, six, two, one, three*, and attempts to repeat this sequence without error. It is noteworthy for us that the classic paradigm of this experiment is a linguistic task: the participant perceives speech (or reads it) and then produces speech in turn. Serial recall is a controlled linguistic exercise.

Serial recall has been extensively researched over the last seventy years, and a model of serial recall and serial order today must meet a large number of empirical constraints to be a viable model. Because many factors have been shown to affect serial recall performance, detecting a new one requires very careful stimulus construction and control (for a recent review, see Hitch, Hurlstone, & Hartley, 2022). For this work, we will skip directly towards influential models that will push our discussion of time in language forward.

2.1 Competitive Queuing

One key mechanism used in a variety of serial order models is competitive queuing (Bohland, Bullock, & Guenther, 2010; Burgess & Hitch, 1992, 1999, 2006; Grossberg, 1978; Houghton & Hartley, 1995; Lewandowsky & Farrell, 2008). With competitive queuing, several items are all activated in parallel and then 'compete' to be selected. Competition includes each item exciting itself – trying to increase its own activation – and inhibiting its competitors – lowering their activations. Which one will win? In general, the winning candidate will be the one that is most active at the start, because that one has more energy to out-compete the other candidates. The leading candidate's own activity increases while it inhibits its competitors' activity. When the competitor reaches a threshold, the item is **selected** and initiates. For instance, if the competing items were a set of words, then one word would win and be uttered.

However, if the process stopped here, then the winner would be selected in perpetuity, endlessly being re-selected. To say the second word, which had a lower starting activation than the first, we must get the first one out of its way. This happens through a **suppression** process. After an item passes the thresh-old, a feedback mechanism strongly suppresses its activation so that it plummets to a level smaller than the competitors. This gives space for the second most active item to be selected. This process repeats as long as there are active items (Figure 1).

Competitive queuing then could be a deterministic process: the order of selection is determined entirely by the activation levels of the items at each time point. Noise in activation levels can disrupt this, however. If the noise, or randomness, is very low, then almost every selection will be determined by the specified activity levels at the start. With increased noise, it becomes possible for a less active candidate to get a random boost over a more active one.

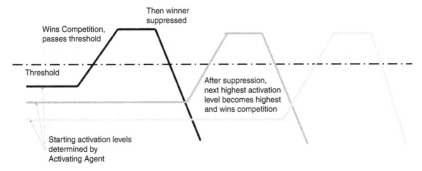

Figure 1 Schematic representation of three items in competitive queuing

Noise then becomes a source of error. If the goal of the competitive queuing model is to model human behaviour, this error becomes a virtue. Errors are a primary guide to discover the sort of factors that guide a speaker's mental models. For instance, errors that switch out the beginnings of words can be evidence that beginnings are a constituent, to use a linguistic concept. Similarly, more errors on items in the beginning of a sequence than on the first item in a sequence gives further evidence of how our mind is handling sequences. A strong psychological model generates the sorts of errors that humans in fact make and avoids generating errors they do not make (Hurlstone, 2021). With competitive queuing, we have a system where activation levels of competing items determine what will be selected. What determines those activation levels, though? The activating agent.

To understand this, it might be best to step back and recall the goal. We want to build a model of how a speaker can hear items in a sequence, remember the items and the sequence, and then recall both when prompted. To give a concrete example, they might hear a sequence of numbers:

9   2   8   5   1   3

Two main types of mistake occur when repeating this sequence. The speaker might err about what numbers were said, such as saying '7 2 8 5 1 3' when no 7 was present in the heard sequence. This would be an **item error**. The speaker also might make an **order error**, such as saying, '2 9 8 5 1 3', which switches the first two items in the sequence but includes all the correct items. Therefore, models have two primary components.

Component One represents the items. This could be a simple representation like using the exact number symbols, but it could be more complex as well. To take an example, let us say we want to create an item representation for the word *spoon*. We could use phonemic symbols:

s   p   ʉː   n

The entire word is represented with a vector of four dimensions, one dimension for each phoneme. A limitation to this representation is that it has no notion of phonetic similarity. This does not match empirical evidence. *Spoon* and *spool* are confused more often than *spoon* and *cheese*. To model facts such as this, researchers can introduce a phonetic characterisation into the item representation. One solution would be to break each phoneme apart into pseudo-features:

s ➜	alveolar	voiceless	frication	unrounded
p ➜	bilabial	voiceless	plosive	rounded
ʉː ➜	palatal	voiced	vowel	rounded
n ➜	alveolar	voiced	nasal	unrounded

This represents each sound with a four-dimensional vector (which is of course partial), needing the full 4x4 array to represent a word. With this more complex representation, sounds that share more features would be confused more often than sounds that share few features. If a model with the posited phonetic representation produces results similar to actual speakers, then it is taken as evidence that people might indeed use that representation.

Component Two is a representation of the order, often called the context or learning context because it is the context in which the items are heard. For a repetition experiment, we want to store the context of the items and then repeat those items based upon the context. Therefore, it is this **context signal**, which is the activating agent. The context signal will set the activation levels for the items for competitive queuing. Many different models therefore can use competitive queuing as the selection mechanism but change the context signal to better match empirical results of speaker behaviour. In our next sections, we will examine a model that uses a dynamic system in the form of cascading oscillators to represent the context signal. To deal with this model, we first need to look at what a dynamic system and oscillator are.

2.2 Dynamic Systems and Oscillators

A dynamic system is any system that changes states over time (Figure 2). A traffic signal can be interpreted as a dynamic system with three states. At time t_1, it has a state of green; at time t_2, a state of yellow; and at time t_3 a state of red.[2] Green, yellow, and red are its **states** or **state space**.

---

[2] We are ignoring other states such as flashing versions of the colour. Moves back to a colour in a sequence do not change what the possible states are, only the sequence of those states.

Figure 2 Examples of three systems, each with a state space. The traffic light has three possible states, the coin has two possible states per coin, and the dice have six states per die. Expressed differently, the light has a state space of {green, yellow, red}, the coin a state space of {heads, tails}, and a die a state space of {1, 2, 3, 4, 5, 6}.

The state space is the collection of states that something can be in. In the traffic light example, the three colours are the only possible states. All three can occur and no additional states ever occur. A coin can have two states: heads or tails. There are no other options for it. In common dynamic systems terminology, if you were to call heads when someone flips a coin, you are 'predicting an outcome in the coin's state space'. In a role-playing game, you might find dice with varying numbers of sides: 4, 6, 8, 10, 12, 20, and so on. Each of these dice then has a state space of 4, 6, 8, and so on. A fair coin or die have equal odds for each of its states, but this need not be the case. A traffic light usually spends much less time on yellow than on red or green. Therefore, when driving up to a light, the probability that its state is yellow is lower than the probability of red or green. Dynamic systems' state spaces are combinations of the possible states and the probability of each.

Another common type of dynamic system is represented by clocks and pendulums. A mechanical analogue clock also has a state space, the times on the clock. As a first approximation, we can say that its states are one, two, three, and so on. The states of the clock evolve over time and can be described with a set of equations, lacking the randomness of a sequence of coin flips. Something special happens when eleven turns into twelve, however, because that twelve o'clock is the same state the clock started from. What clocks measure, time itself, moves on so that this afternoon's twelve o'clock is not this morning's twelve o'clock, much less yesterday's or last year's. However, the clock itself has no state to represent this. Its only states are the times on the clock. The clock loses all information that cannot be represented in its states. Clocks repeat their states with a certain **period**, a period of twelve hours.

Periods should be familiar from the study of acoustic phonetics. A voice with a fundamental frequency of 100 Hz repeats a pattern of amplitude fluctuations 100 times in a second. A transformation of the complex wave of speech into sine wave components finds the frequencies of each simple wave. All of these are examples of dynamic systems that move repeatedly through the same states and are called **oscillators**.

Understanding an oscillator requires two more critical parameters. The first is amplitude. Sound can oscillate at the same frequency with different amplitude, a measure of the energy in the system. The second parameter is the oscillator's phase. Phase is where in the period the system is. For a clock, it could be at one, two, and so on. Because phase indicates the states of the oscillator, all the possible phases of a clock are its **phase space**. Phase is frequently measured in degrees or radians around the circle. Phase space can be continuous, where any phase can be made infinitely precise. In practice, physical oscillators will have a resolution limit. An hour hand, for instance, is not very useful to time competitors in a swim meet, because the difference between winning and losing can be a fraction of a second and an hour hand is poor at displaying that level of temporal precision. This resolution limit may be inherent in the system itself (a system with discrete steps) or a limit to our ability to measure the system (a continuous system that we can only measure discretely).

2.3 OSCAR Serial Order Model

We are now ready to put item and context representations from competitive queuing together with a dynamic system to create the oscillator-based associate recall (OSCAR; Brown, Preece, & Hulme, 2000) computational model for serial recall. The central innovation of OSCAR is that it proposes a set of dynamic oscillators as the context signal to be the activating agent for competitive queuing (Figure 3). The item representation uses a sixteen-item phonetic vector to represent each item. The learning context also uses a vector, but rather than modelling phonetic similarity, it needs to model temporal similarity of items. First, a set of fifteen different oscillators is created. Each oscillator has a different frequency so that there are 'fast' and 'slow' oscillators to cover different timescales of the experiment. This provides something like a hierarchical representation since fast oscillators are nested within slower ones at multiple levels. The product of these oscillators (using their cosine and sine representations) is then calculated to create the final learning context vector. This is similar to taking two simple sound waves and combining them to form a complex wave, though

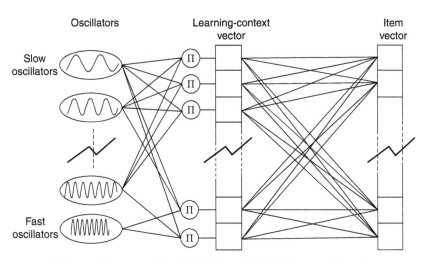

Figure 3 The architecture of the OSCAR model. The item and learning context vectors are paired on the right of the figure. On the left, a set of cascaded oscillators are multiplied to generate the learning context signal. Reprinted with permission (Brown, Preece, & Hulme, 2000, p. 131, figure 5).

a product is used rather than a sum. Rather than being a sound, however, the result is the context representation for serial recall.

During serial recall, the first procedure in the model pairs the researcher-created item vector with the context vector, modelling hearing the sequence and learning the context. The item and context oscillators progress from state to state together. Because the learning context is made from oscillators at different speeds, each step in time can potentially have a different 'look', or amplitude profile, in the same way that multiple acoustic waves can generate a distinct 'look'. In a step where multiple oscillators interfere with each other, they create a context signal without distinctive landmarks. At other steps, multiple oscillators will coincide with their direction up or down, making a sharp, distinctive profile. A distinct profile creates a clearer match between the context and the item.

The second procedure in OSCAR uses the learning context to recall the items, modelling the steps in which items are produced. The learning context signal is replayed and items that best match the pairing are recalled. The OSCAR model is able to reproduce several patterns in human serial recall, successfully recalling items and reproducing error patterns from human participants. The first OSCAR model simulated recalling word-like items in a sequence. It has been extended to model the productions of phonemes in a sequence when speaking. We turn to the study of sequencing in speech production now.

2.4 From Serial Order to Speech Production

The classic serial recall task focused on how to reproduce a stimulus like a series of digits in the right order. However, saying the name of the digit 3 requires producing the phonemes /θ/, /ɹ/, and /i/ in the right order as well. Serial order is a part of the phonological representations of words. Mistakes that can occur in reproducing a list of digits resemble speech errors one can make: the speaker may insert a phoneme that is not in the word, delete a phoneme that is in the word, or say phonemes in the wrong order. Using the terms from serial recall study, insertions and deletions would be item errors, and a phoneme sequencing error would be an order error.

Target:	[θɹi]
Insertion error:	[θɹit̪]
Deletion error:	[ɹi]
Order error:	[θiɹ]

If we conceive of speaking as a question of placing the items of language in the right sequence, then we might build a model of speaking with the components of serial order models: an item representation, an order or learning context representation, competitive queuing, and so on.

One possible mechanism for representing items and order would be to have a set of frames to slot items into (Figure 4). The frame provides the order for the items. In one of the earliest models, Shattuck-Hufnagel (1979) proposed a dual representation for speech production, with (1) slots to fill and (2) target phonemes to fill them. During production, phonemes are copied into their target slots so that they are produced in the right order.[3] Such a step implies (1) the existence of a mechanism that performs this matching (which Shattuck-Hufnagel calls the scan-copier) and (2) that the mechanism itself has some set of 'rules' of what to do. Several models follow a slot-filler model (Dell, 1986; Roelofs, 1997; Shattuck-Hufnagel, 1979; Turk & Shattuck-Hufnagel, 2020). One possible frame is that of phonological prosody. Phonemes map to syllables, which map to larger prosodic units. In Figure 4, the phonemes are filled into the prosodic slots of syllable structure. In the terms of serial order mechanisms, prosody becomes the learning context representation and phonemes are the item representation.

A general issue that can arise with such models is an 'it's turtles all the way down' problem. Specifically, if there is a system X that takes items and places them into slots using labels, what controls system X? If a system Y 'reads' the

---

[3] The slot-filler draws again on the spatial metaphor of language as objects being put in a place in space.

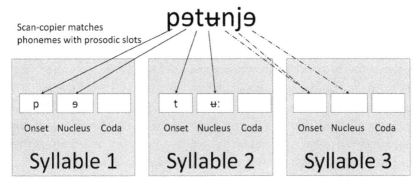

Figure 4 A simplified model of a slot-filler ordering mechanism where phonemes are inserted into slots of a prosodic frame.

labels for X, what controls Y? And Z? This might have a direct, grounded answer, terminating the question. We have not looked at any of these proposed models in sufficient detail to determine whether a regress happens, but one way to avoid this is to establish some mechanical process that can directly drive an action when it is needed.[4] This is one motivation for Vousden, Brown, and Harley (2000), who do not use a slot-filler model, but instead borrow the context signal from OSCAR and apply it to phonological production.

Like OSCAR for serial recall, there are two components: the item representation and the context representation. The item representation uses a set of phonological features, rather than phonemes directly. This makes it possible to represent item similarity in terms of features. Items that are similar, such as /p/ and /b/, will then be more likely to be confused in production, which is what actual speakers do. Also, like OSCAR, the learning context is the product of a set of oscillators of varying speeds. One modification to OSCAR for serial recall is explicitly making some oscillators repeating and some non-repeating. An example (from Vousden et al., 2000) might make the difference clear.

For the word subjective /sʌb.dʒek.tɪv/,[5] there are three syllables and three phonemes per syllable. Using the clock analogue, the hour hand could represent the syllables. Moving from one hour to the next, the hours do not repeat during this sequence. Each syllable is distinct. The minute hand, however, could represent the syllable position (onset, nucleus, coda). Each position repeats within each successive syllable: [s] is the onset for syllable one and [dʒ] for

---

[4] We also return to this question, which I call the homunculus problem, in the Conclusion.

[5] This transcript replicates the one from Vousden and colleagues' (2000) article rather than New Zealand English.

syllable two. There is positional similarity between adjacent phonemes, but there is also similarity across syllables for each syllable position. Where there is similarity, there is an increased chance of switching items as an error.

Rather than two clock hands, Vousden and colleagues (2000) use a set of thirty oscillators, fifteen repeating ones and fifteen non-repeating ones, varying in frequency. Each oscillator is represented as a sine wave that rotates through its phase space with a certain period. For a simulation, the oscillator starts at a particular phase angle and then steps to the next phase angle at each point in time. By varying the size of the step, the oscillators can model different speech rates.

The process of (1) learning the phonological sequence and (2) speaking the sequence works quite similarly to OSCAR for serial recall. During learning, both the item representation and the phonological context occur at once so that the two can be paired. When speaking, the oscillators-as-phonological-context are then initiated. As the phonological context steps through its dynamic representation, the items most closely matching that context during learning are recalled. If a step in the phonological context is entirely distinct from all other steps, then the matching item can be retrieved. If, however, that step is similar to other steps, then it might be unclear which item to recall, and an error is possible. Increased noise can also trigger speech errors. The OSCAR-based model of phonological production succeeds in generating speech in the right order as well as producing errors that are common.

Let us quickly review where we are in the Element. We want to know if focusing on the dimension of time in speech will change how we think of phonology and phonetics. The time question focused on so far has been the one of serial order. We want to know how we remember when to take linguistic actions so that they occur in the right order. This look at existing dynamic theories has introduced some terms uncommon in structural linguistics. We have not reflected these concepts back on phonology yet, except to note that serial order is an implicit part of any phonological representation. We will continue our selective journey into dynamic models of speech production for a while longer before turning back to phonology. Our next step is to examine the approach known as articulatory phonology.

3 Speech Production

3.1 Articulatory Phonology and the Task Dynamic Toolkit

Arguably, the most comprehensive theory of speech production that tracks all the way from a phonological representation of a word to detailed modelling and prediction of speech articulation, including precise durations, is that of articulatory phonology as paired with the task dynamic toolkit (henceforth AP/TD). Turk and Shattuck-Hufnagel (2020), who spend an entire monograph critiquing and constructing an alternative to AP/TD, still state that AP/TD sets the standard for comprehensiveness of speech production models (p. 1) and that it is this model's explicitness that allowed them to develop their differing approach (p. 320.)

The core idea of articulatory phonology is that the phonological representation of lexemes is built in articulatory terms (i.e., the phonological representation contains information about speech gestures). This is a radical shift from the phoneme-based structural linguistics this Element assumed at the start. Phonological representations are made from 'gestural atoms' rather than phonemes (Browman & Goldstein, 1989, p. 201). Within AP/TD, a gesture is derived from familiar articulatory gestures like tongue movements, but AP/TD gestures do not equate directly to motor movements. Rather, gestures are defined in terms of **tract variables**, which define the location and degrees of constriction of the vocal tract. Key tract variables include:

- Lip aperture (LA)
- Lip protrusion (LP)
- Tongue tip (TT)
- Tongue body (TB)
- Velic aperture (VA)
- Glottal aperture (GA)

As examples, lip aperture indicates the opening the two lips, and velic aperture is the opening when the velum is lowered to allow nasality. Many of these variables are in fact separated into multiple parameters, often location and degree. So, Tongue Tip (TT) is not a single tract variable. Instead, there is Tongue Tip Constriction Location (TTCL) and Tongue Tip Constriction Degree (TTCD). The location would indicate if a sound were alveolar, post-alveolar, and so on. Degree would indicate a full closure, such as for plosive stops, or a partial closure, such as for fricatives (Browman & Goldstein, 1986, 1989). To make this concrete, for many English speakers, a [d] would involve a tongue tip gesture that sets the tongue tip constriction and location tract variables to evolve towards a full closure at the alveolar ridge. A gesture that would result in a [k] would drive tongue body constriction and location variables toward a velar closure.

Some aspects of this are familiar from articulatory phonetics, but there are two key differences. First, this is articulatory *phonology*. There is no process wherein symbolic amodal phonemes must be phonetically realised in articulatory terms. Phonemes as lexical representation are replaced by gestures so that they are already inherently articulatory. AP/TD can still use segments and speak of a [t] or [k], but these are viewed as practical tools, not how the phonological system is cognitively organised. Second, active gestures drive movement as an evolving process. An active gesture pushes a tract variable towards a certain value over time (Byrd, 1996; Tilsen, 2019b). Therefore, they can be thought of as a source of energy or a force pushing another element of the system. We will return to this concept later in the Element.

Sounds frequently are not composed of the activity from single gestures, but rather the **coordination** of multiple gestures in time. For instance, a fully voiced [d] would require both a tongue tip gesture and a glottal adduction gesture[6]. Similarly, a voiceless [t] would require both a tongue tip gesture and a glottal spread gesture. Gestures can be placed into sequences as well. So [da] could have a beginning tongue tip gesture with glottal vibration, followed by the ending (release) of the tongue tip gesture while glottal vibration continues. A [ta], however would only have a change to a glottal vibration gesture occurring after the tongue tip gesture is released. A [tʰ] would have some delay between ending the tongue tip gesture and initiating the glottal gesture. If one thinks of the activation intervals of gestures as note times/durations, and the tract variables as note qualities (i.e., C, D#, etc.), then one can arrange them in a **gestural score** (Figures 5a and 5b).

We can compare this to our serial order discussion before. There, a word's phonology was assumed to be a set of phonemes and an order. Gestural scores

Generic Gestural Score

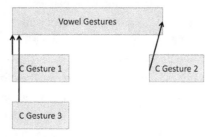

Figure 5a A generic gestural score where consonantal gestures are coordinated with vowel gestures. Each rectangle represents a period of time in which a tract variable is active to drive articulator motion. An arrow indicates a timing coordination.

---

[6] In AP/TD, voicing is, however, the default state and does not require a gesture.

Gestural Score for [sʉːn] *soon*

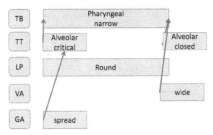

Figure 5b A gestural score for the word *soon*. Tongue tip and glottal gestures are coordinated with the start of a tongue body gesture. Alveolar and velar gestures are coordinated with the end of the tongue body gesture. Terms like narrow, critical and closed refer to constriction degree. Abbreviations such as TT, TB, and so on refer to tract variables as discussed in the text.

are models of dynamic systems sending energy at different points in time to create action. AP/TD also challenges serial order as the mechanism for coordinating actions in speech. Gestures are not objects that must be placed one after the other in a line. They can generate forces, and forces can overlap in time, boosting or interfering with each other.

Within AP/TD, allophonic processes are created through the interactions of gestures. Insertion, assimilation, and deletion of sounds – which would be written as rules or constraints in phonological grammars – occur because of gestural changes. Figure 6 shows a gestural score for the word *prune* where [ɹ] becomes devoiced after a voiceless sound. The activation of the glottal spread gesture of the voiceless [p] continues past the end of the lip gesture and overlaps extensively with the tongue tip gesture. The result is a devoiced [ɹ]. The assimilation results from a change in timing of gestures.

Gestural scores can also handle some insertions and deletions. For example, take a pattern like Thomson → Thom[p]son. In a phonological rule, this would be written as the insertion of a [p] in a certain phonetic environment. In a gestural score, this would be accounted for again by changing the timing of gestures. In this case, a velic gesture (nasalisation) coordinated with a bilabial constriction creates an [m]. When this velic gesture ends before the release of the bilabial constriction, paired with the glottal opening gesture, it results in a [p]. The [p] has been 'inserted' via gestural timing. An apparent deletion can occur in a similar manner. When the timing of a gesture hides the presence of another gesture, it can sound as if it has been deleted. Therefore, inserting, deleting, and assimilating sounds are all accomplished through the coordination of gestures as expressed in a gestural score. This system will struggle, however,

Gestural score for [pɹ̥ʉːn] *prune*

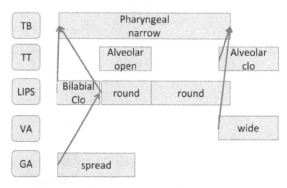

Figure 6 A gestural score for the word *prune*. The critical portion of this score is the spread glottis represented at the bottom. The glottal gesture continues past the end of the lip gesture over much of the alveolar gesture.

to express morphophonological alternations such as electri[k] → electri[s]ity. In this change, an entirely different gesture must be made: an alveolar tongue tip versus a velar tongue body gesture. One might argue that this is a morphophonological change and AP/TD only describes pure phonology. However, this would reintroduce non-gestural representations of the forms of words, requiring translation of non-gestural representations into gestural representations. AP/TD is intended to remove the necessity of this, not simply push it back further into the morphology. Morphophonology therefore remains an open problem for AP/TD.

Despite its merits, a gestural score does not yet build a comprehensive model of articulation from phonological representation to motor control. The gestures set goals for tract variables but, by themselves, do not model how they are in fact realised. The task dynamic approach tackles questions like this (Saltzman & Byrd, 2000; Saltzman & Munhall, 1989; Saltzman, Nam, Krivokapic, & Goldstein, 2008). The task dynamic approach takes a set of tasks from the gestural score and then models how those tasks drive movement (i.e., changes in vocal tract variables), as a dynamic system. The system it models is an oscillator: that of a mass on a spring whose movement is damped.

Imagine a block attached to the end of a spring. If you stretch the spring and then release it, it will bounce for some amount of time before coming to a rest. If the spring has a force stopping its movement, it will not bounce for long. This amount of suppression is its damping. If a spring has a high damping parameter, it might only move out once before all motion is stopped. Thinking of tract variables for the tongue tip, the speech goal is to move the tip to some location at a particular time and then stop so that, for instance, a [d] is pronounced. In AP/ TD then, the tongue would be analogous to a damped spring.

The change in tract variables can be modelled with this spring and attached mass. If a spring starts at some resting location and the mass is pulled, the distance between the home position and its current position is its displacement. Change in the mass's displacement over time comprises its velocity. Objects cannot go from no movement to moving with a constant velocity instantaneously. They speed up and slow down. This change in velocity is an object's acceleration. In total, the movement of a mass on a spring can be modelled with the following parameters:

- the natural frequency of the spring
- the damping of the spring
- the displacement of the spring
- the velocity of the spring
- the acceleration of the spring
- the force on the spring as it changes over time.

A second-order dynamic equation models this. To explain: velocity is the change in location over time. In calculus, rate of change is modelled with derivatives, so velocity is the first derivative of displacement. Acceleration is change in velocity over time (speeding up, slowing down), so acceleration is the derivative of velocity or the second derivative of displacement. Since the highest derivative within this dynamic system is acceleration, the second derivative, this is a second-order dynamical system.

We have worked through all of this to convey what the task dynamic toolkit is doing. It takes a set of tasks as provided by the gestural score of low-dimensional resolution and turns them into high-dimensional actions for the motor system. It models the shift from a qualitative description such as 'tongue tip moves to the alveolar ridge' to a quantitative specification of motion through time and space.

Articulatory phonology is best known for making phonology out of gestures, but we are covering it in this Element because of how embedded time is within the theory.

- Gestures exert forces for a duration of time.
- Consonants and vowels may emerge because of how gestures are coordinated in time.
- Phonological processes are created by changes in the timing of gestures.
- Phonologically contrastive representations depart from a spatial metaphor – phoneme blocks stacked in a row – to a more temporal one with forces in time.

For AP/TD, timing is not a follow-up question for those interested in detailed phonetics; it is part of the phonological representation of a word. 'Words are composed of an ensemble of gestures, organized in time in a particular fashion' (Goldstein et al., 2009, p. 1). But what is the timing mechanism for all of this? AP/TD proposes a now familiar answer here: oscillators, specifically **coupled oscillators**.[7]

To understand coupling, it could be helpful to explore everyday experiences of oscillators. A musical rhythm is oscillatory with repeating patterns in time. Similarly, tapping a foot to a rhythm is also oscillatory, where the foot taps at a particular beat (i.e., period). If you tap your foot to the beat of the music, you now have two coupled oscillators. The foot is entrained to the music, where the foot's oscillation (period and phase) is matched to the music's oscillation. Since the music is external to the person tapping their foot, foot-tapping to music is a case of extrinsic entrainment. If a person were tapping their foot to music in their head, that would be intrinsic entrainment, since both rhythms are generated by the person's mind. Extrinsic and intrinsic are defined relative to some system.

Importantly for the AP/TD model, entrainment can take on other forms than always tapping on the beat. Generally, in human performance, there are two stable ways for entrainment to occur: (1) in-phase and (2) anti-phase. Take the rhythm:

One   and   two   and   three   and   four   and

where the primary oscillation is the repeating 'number-and' sequence. Tapping in-phase would look like this (where the tap is indicated with **bold** font).

One   and   **two**   and   **three**   and   **four**   and

while tapping anti-phase would look like this

one   **and**   two   **and**   three   **and**   four   **and**

This takes a precise meaning if you define the period precisely.

In Figure 7, the *one* occurs at the top of the period (circle), while the *and* occurs at the bottom. The phase is indicated with 0 at the top and 1/2 at the bottom. If the phase is expressed in degrees, the top would be 0 degrees and the bottom 180 degrees. If expressed in radians, then the top is 0 and the bottom is π. A complete entrainment matches the phase in one oscillator to the phase in another oscillator.

---

[7] OSCAR also uses coupled oscillators, but it was possible to defer explanation of coupling to this point.

Figure 7 A clock as oscillator with the two most stable points for human entrainment indicated, 0 and ½.

AP/TD uses coupled oscillators to coordinate gestures. This coupling is less like a person tapping to a metronome and more like two people tapping with each other. Both systems are actively phase-shifting to match one another. Gestures that are coupled in-phase (both occur on the *one*) initiate at the same time. In a CV syllable, the consonant and vowel gestures can often initiate at the same time and so are in-phase. In a VC syllable, however, the consonantal gesture must follow the initiation of the vowel gesture. This is accomplished by having the C in an anti-phase relationship with the V. A CVC syllable in turn combines both an in-phase coupling for the CV part and an anti-phase coupling for the VC. How about a more complex syllable structure such as CCVC? In this case, the gestures of the consonant cluster are anti-phase, ensuring that one comes before the other. AP/TD then does not use a selection mechanism for serial order, but instead oscillator-based coordination.

Put together then, AP/TD is a coherent system that specifies a phonological representation of words, how allophonic processes occur, and how the articulators move in time and space. Whether we use articulatory phonology and the task dynamic toolkit or a different theory, some bridge must be built between categorical-seeming phonology and highly specific, varying motor control. Phonemes, features, or gestural scores must become actual events in time with specific durations. An utterance may have a structure but it is also an event in time.

While the comprehensiveness of AP/TD certainly deserves appreciation, many might wonder if it sacrifices too much of well-earned linguistic theory. Phonemes, processes, constraints, all of these have decades of research supporting them (for recent defences of the phoneme, see Bowers, Kazanina, & Andermane, 2016; Kazanina et al., 2018; Fowler, Shankweiler, & Studdert-Kennedy, 2016, but for disagreement, see Boucher, 2021; Samuel, 2020). Is it possible to develop a similarly comprehensive model of speech that starts with phonemes but ends with specific time and velocity predictions of articulators? Turk and Shattuck-Hufnagel (2020) set out to do just that.

3.2 Speech Production without Oscillators

According to Turk and Shattuck-Hufnagel (2020), the AP/TD approach sets the 'standard' (p. 8) for speech production. However, they believe it has fundamental flaws and have started the development of an alternate approach. One reason for us to spend substantial time with Turk and Shattuck-Hufnagel's theory is that observations and predictions about durations are critical for their theoretical development. Many of the innovations of their model are based upon what they see as incorrect temporal predictions or flawed temporal modelling. These include the following:

1. Extensive motor control research has discovered a systematic relationship between distance of a movement, spatial accuracy of that movement, and the duration of that movement, a relationship known as Fitts' Law. For a movement to keep the same spatial accuracy, its duration increases with distance. AP/TD does not include spatial accuracy as a goal of the system and therefore does not express Fitts' Law.
2. Often, distinct tasks that are done at the same time interfere with each other. A classic common example is difficulty patting your head and rubbing your stomach. AP/TD utilises synchronous actions as a design feature with no indication of interference.
3. Many factors influence durational movements. This means, according to Turk and Shattuck-Hufnagel, that we need a planning system that can manage and optimise the accomplishment of many goals. AP/TD uses a default durational pattern with adjustments that could struggle to handle such a complex interweaving of goals. Indeed, the 'default' may rarely surface due to the pervasiveness of these multiple goals.
4. Additionally, it is the temporal *endpoints* of movements that are often the most carefully controlled and timed. The end of the movement will often have the smallest variation in realisation, while beginning and medial points have greater variation, suggesting that the end point is the target. Speaking informally, it does not matter when you leave on the trip as long as you arrive on time. This is a problem for AP/TD because their system coordinates the *initiation* of movements as the target, not the endpoint.

All this evidence is introduced by Turk and Shattuck-Hufnagel to argue that AP/TD has fundamental theoretical errors and therefore new work is needed. Their alternative system is called the **phonology-extrinsic-timing-based three-component (XT/3C)** model. The three components are (see also Figure 8):

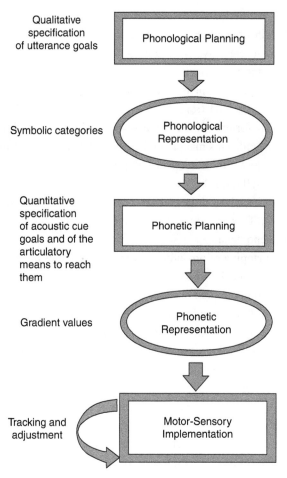

Figure 8 The overall architecture of the XT/3C model. Reprinted with permission (Turk & Shattuck-Hufnagel, 2020, p. 188, figure 7.3.

1. phonological planning
2. phonetic planning
3. motor-sensory implementation.

We will not cover all of the motivation and detail of the model but provide a basic sketch (Their own sketch is primarily in Chapter 10).

First, the Phonological Planning component has several pieces: (1) a symbolic, phonemic representation of lexical entries, (2) a planning component for prosodic structure, and (3) a set of context-specific qualitative and relational acoustic cues. This phonological model purposefully does not include a timing model of the gestures to be made. It includes a prosodic framework that will have temporal repercussions, but the component includes no durational predictions. This is the meaning of 'phonology-extrinsic-timing' and is in opposition to AP/TD, where phonological gestures have timing intrinsic to early systems. During phonological planning, phonemes are placed into the prosodic frames like a slot-filler model of serial order, covered previously. Next, the prosodic frame filled with phonemes is mapped to acoustic goals, derived from the work of Stevens (2002). Example goals might be a certain formant pattern for a vowel, a silence from a full closure, or a reduction in sound. This mapping takes the prosodic frame in mind, so that a /t/ is mapped to a strong burst in one prosodic context (such as the start of a stressed syllable) but to a reduced or absent burst in another prosodic context (such as at the end of a prosodic word where the /t/ is lightly or un-released). This mapping then is quite detailed, taking into account a number of phenomena.

Indeed, this mapping of prosodically framed phonemes to acoustic goals is one of the largest contributions of their model (see also Guenther, 2016). First, note that it is partially implementing what phonological grammars like phono-logical rules or OT are intended to do. The mapping changes abstract categor-ies to more specific realisations based on prosody and context. Phonological patterns such as aspiration or final lengthening are planned within this map-ping of phonemes to acoustic landmarks. Handling allophonic-like patterns here is not shocking: This is called the phonological component of the model. However, using phoneme to acoustic landmark mapping is not the way that dominant phonological theories model these changes. In XT/3C creating acoustic goals happens *before* sending to the phonetic component for detailed articulation. The closest parallel in existing theory might be optimality-theoretic models that embed phonetics into the grammar (Boersma, 1998; Kirchner, 1998). However, XT/3C intentionally separates phonetic planning from phonological planning. Turk and Shattuck-Hufnagel discuss these models of OT when comparing their *phonetic* component to existing models, not their *phonological* component.

Once the mapping to acoustic landmarks is complete, the information is passed to the phonetic planning component (Figure 8). The primary task in phonetic planning is to take categorical information from the phonology and turn it into scalar, quantifiable values. It is here where actual durations can be specified, as well as other quantified values such as intensity, pitch, and so on. As Turk and Shattuck-Hufnagel put it, 'The goal of the Phonetic Planning Component is to determine values of phonetic parameters that will produce appropriate landmarks and other feature-relevant cues to signal the sequence of segments/contrastive elements in its prosodic frame, while appropriately meet-ing the prioritized list of other task requirements for the utterance' (pp. 298–9).

Because the intention is to map multiple qualitative goals into multiple quantitative goals that can be implemented in muscle movements, the authors borrow optimal control theory (OCT) from the study of motor control. OCT works by optimising a cost function. A set of goals and a set of costs are specified. The maths of OCT generate a plan that minimises the costs and maximises the achievement of goals. Among the costs that XT/3C considers are effort, time, and the cost of not meeting a goal. Turk and Shattuck-Hufnagel do not attempt to specify all parameters of the OCT control policy that would be needed, conceding that some differing costs can be difficult to distinguish as they make similar predictions.

The third component of XT/3C is the motor-sensory implementation (Figure 8), which takes a now quantified optimal control policy and implements it. While the phonetic components contained quantified temporal targets, it is only in the third component that an actual timing mechanism is called on. Turk and Shattuck-Hufnagel do not use oscillators for their timing system, but instead general tau theory (Lee, 1998). Tau is the time it would take to close an existing gap if gap closure continued at the current movement rate (p. 256). Tau goals are set during phonetic planning and then implemented during motor-sensory implementation. Timing is implemented by coupling two measures of tau, such as a tau-goal and the current tau-value. This system assumes that a model of movement can predict what the tau should be so that actual muscle movement can couple to it. Models using general tau theory generate movement profiles similar to empirically observed movement and in some measures better match those movements than AP/TD's predictions. General tau theory then also works by coupling systems together; however, while AP/TD couples multiple oscillator systems, general tau theory couples different time-varying taus.

The goal for this Element is not to determine the ideal model of speech production. Rather, we want to understand how language is viewed differently when time is taken into consideration. With the development of the XT/3C model, we see a wide impact of taking time data seriously. Attempting to account for observed durations has created a version of phonology not seen before. AP/TD wanted a theory that could move all the way from gestural categories to actual durations, and the result was the incorporation of oscillators and temporally specified gestures right into the phonology. XT/3C argues that timing should not be embedded in the phonology but external to it. This then requires a mapping between atemporal symbols and temporal movement goals. The theory performs this translation by mapping symbols to qualitative and relational acoustic and duration goals in the phonology, which can then be mapped to quantified temporal goals in phonetic planning and finally an implementation of those temporal goals in motor control. Therefore, the requirement to consider time has generated a new conception of phonology, even when the theory maintains that symbolic phonemes are the primary phonological structure of lexical items.

It is worth noting how concepts familiar from OT appear in both the phonological and phonetic planning components of XT/3C. The phonological mapping of phonemes to acoustic landmarks is reminiscent of phonetically-based OT, where acoustic goals can become constraints. And, as Turk and Shattuck-Hufnagel discuss extensively (chapter 8), their use of OCT is also reminiscent of OT in that both attempt to find an optimal solution to a set of costs or constraints. Altogether, this raises the question: Does OT often succeed because it approximates the more comprehensive XT/3C? Answering this is far beyond the scope of this work. However, again, building a theory that explicitly deals with time changes how one theorises about language beyond simple predictions of time. In the case of AP/TD, you end up with a phonological theory made of gestures, oscillatory systems, and dynamic spring models. In the case of XT/3C, you end up with a phonological theory where even the phonological component has a bridge built in to enable future durational goals to be specified. Either way, the conception of basic linguistic structures has changed, so it does not seem right to think of AP/TD or XT/3C as implementation details.

3.3 Summarising Speech Production So Far

This text has covered three primary theories of speech production:

1. OSCAR-based speech production: Memory stores an association between phonological items and an oscillator-based context. To speak, the oscillator context drives the selection of items.
2. AP/TD: An oscillator-based context drives the coordination of gesture-based tract variable tasks. These coordinated tasks then drive the motion of articulators as a dynamic system.
3. XT/3C: Among other things, memory contains lexical items and possible prosodic structures, the general tau theory equation, and a set of optimisation procedures. Prosodically slotted phonemes are connected to a set of acoustic goals. The best way to implement these competing goals is determined using general tau theory and OCT.

Each theory has particular strengths, fitting some data and not others, and each has gaps other theories fill. Looking broadly across the approaches, however, we see some shared elements:

1. Each approach specifies the <u>items</u> that must be <u>coordinated</u> in time.
2. Each approach <u>selects</u> particular items to be produced.
3. Each approach has one or more <u>control</u> mechanisms that allow for selection and coordination.
4. Each approach specifies the <u>goals</u> for production.

The phonological component of XT/3C *selects* phonemes as *items* for production and determines acoustic *goals* for those phonemes and then delivers them to optimal *control* theory to plan articulations for implementation. The phonological component of AP/TD uses a set of oscillators to *control* and *coordinate* the gestures as *items* in a gestural score where the *goals* are embedded in the oscillators, score, and tract variables. The OSCAR model uses oscillators to *select, coordinate,* and *control* the production of phonological feature vectors as *items*. These five elements (items, selection, coordination, control, and goals) are not always distinct. The control mechanism frequently determines which items are selected and coordinated. Some goals could be distinct from the item representation, as timing is distinct in XT/3C but embedded within the item representation, as with AP/TD. Rather, these elements indicate problems that all models must solve.

Despite the progress we have made, there is a glaring gap in our coverage: it is entirely based in production, with little reference to acoustics or audition. The serial order methods of Brown and colleagues (2000) and Vousden and colleagues (2000) only reference hearing as a process to collect the items and learning context but do limited modelling of audition. Articulatory phonology's primary claim is to couch phonology in terms of articulation, putting acoustics to the side. The primary exception to this pattern is the XT/3C model of Turk and Shattuck-Hufnagel (2020), who place acoustic goals directly into the phonological component. To get a fuller picture, we turn to speech perception now.

4 Speech Perception

4.1 Neuronal Oscillations and Speech

Speech perception covers a large range of sub-fields. Sub-fields that examine how we perceive the form of lexical items includes acoustic phonetics, auditory scene analysis, phoneme recognition, word segmentation, word recognition, prosodic processing, and more. Sub-fields that add meaning and processing 'above' the lexicon include morphosyntactic parsing, semantic comprehension, pragmatic processing, and more. Each of these has questions of dynamics and the importance of time in processing. The fact that a primary tool of acoustic phonetics – the spectrogram – includes time indicates that time has been a topic of study for decades. Additionally, speech perception is a 'greedy' process wherein the mind uses information immediately and constantly, rather than gathering all information and then acting. It is a process that is continuous in time. Michael Spivey's *The Continuity of Mind* (Spivey, 2008) reviews much of this information, as do handbook reviews of psycholinguistics (e.g., Spivey, Joanisse, & McRae, 2012). In the few pages here, we will not attempt to address this entire field. Rather, as this Element is about dynamic approaches, we will introduce an approach to speech perception that has gotten a serious look in the literature in the last fifteen years: the role of neuronal oscillations in speech perception (Ghitza, 2011; Luo & Poeppel, 2007; Meyer, 2018; Peele & Davis, 2012).

We might approach this topic by way of comparison to models of word recognition. In the influential TRACE model (McClelland & Elman, 1986), input is encoded via groups of acoustic features. These features are 'pseudo-spectral' parameters such as Voiced, Vocalic, Burst, and Power. These features are input as blocks that change over time. The features then map to phonemes and the phonemes map to words. The TRACE model has various merits, and it has been modified, extended, and critiqued in the three decades since.

A motivation for our current discussion comes from Ghitza (2011), who claims, 'The premise of this study is that current models of speech perception, which are driven by acoustic features alone, are incomplete, and that the role of decoding time during memory access must be incorporated to account for the patterns of observed recognition phenomena' (p. 1). Ghitza is not stating that TRACE in particular is incomplete, but that all such models are incomplete, because they do not consider 'decoding time'. What is this item we need to add to our models? What are these 'observed recognition phenomena'?

Before we can address Ghitza's specific point, we can look at some issues generally that models like TRACE are not built to address:

1. If words (or another unit) are recognised via their acoustic features, how do you know the **order** of those features? We cannot take the order of the acoustic input for granted. Just as speaking requires an output sequence, perception involves an input sequence. If we wish to say *kiss* [kəs], and we in fact say *sick* [sək], that could cause a problem. Similarly, if our conversational partner says [sək] and we hear [kəs], it could become awkward quickly. In other words, our word recognition models with acoustic events as input need some account of how we keep those events in the right order. In computational models like TRACE, the researcher solves this problem by inputting the data in the correct sequence. In natural speech perception, how do we accomplish this (Tune & Obleser, 2022)?

2. If the brain is a continuously active predictor and processor of information, how does that neural activity get matched to the acoustic signal? Putting the question in a more traditional psycholinguistic manner, if the brain uses top-down information (a lexical prediction) and bottom-up information (the acoustic signal), how does the brain know they are about the same thing? The prediction initiates before the data it predicts (or it would not be a <u>pre</u>diction). If one were to predict word X while the acoustics for word Y are arriving, then the two sources of information would confuse each other, not reinforce. It would seem we need some temporal matching process to **bind** the two together (Buzsáki, 2006; di Lollo, 2012; Kandel et al., 2000).

3. In natural environments, we hear a great deal that is not speech concurrently with speech. As I type this, I hear the hum of a heat pump, the breathing of a family member, the taps of my fingers on the keyboard, the taps of another family member on a screen, the sound of sipping tea, and the hum of a motor outside. Some acoustic information is of more value for decoding speech than other information. Human fundamental frequency ranges from about 50 Hz to 600 Hz. The three formants critical for vowels have their own range of just a few thousand Hz. If the areas of our brain that process speech could focus **attention** just on the sound sources and components that relate to speech, that could increase our ability to find the signal in the noise.

In sum, we are looking for some mechanism that can bind our neural processing with the speech signal, as well as one that can help solve the serial order and timing questions of processing the speech signal. Neuronal oscillations could be this mechanism. To understand the proposal, we need to review some basics of how the brain represents information. Our first step is with a single neuron.

A single neuron has a threshold to determine when it will fire.[8] If the electrochemical polarisation of the neuron is below that threshold, it does not fire, but above that threshold it does. Changes in a neuron do occur below the threshold, but the changes do not propagate as a signal to affect a neighbour neuron. Passing the threshold sets off a cascade of electrical activity running the length of a neuron, which then transfers the signal to a neighbour. This change in electrical activity is described as shifting from a resting potential to an action potential. The action potential is frequently spoken of as the neuron 'firing' or

---

[8] This review of key notions from neuroscience is a strong simplification. Spiking pattens vary significantly by neuron type, structural morphology, and more (for a review, see Izhikevich, 2010).

'spiking'. After the neuron spikes, there is a brief time where its electrical balance is reset before it can spike again. The spike of a single neuron then is conceptually similar to the threshold-activation-suppression pattern of competitive queuing, though the mechanics are quite different. The presence of a threshold implies that a single spike is an either/or (True/False) event. A single spike cannot be greater or lesser. The input is sufficient to trigger an action potential, or it is not. Therefore, to have a neural signal that takes a range of values (more detailed than True or False) requires either multiple neurons (a neural population) or a neuron spiking over time, or both. (For accessible introductions to this material, see Kemmerer, 2014; Sedivy, 2019.)

Multiple neurons do allow for a range of activation, because the number of neurons firing can vary. The more neurons fire, the greater the signal from that population of neurons. Sometimes it is useful to convert this to a proportion. If the neural population has 100 neurons and 50 of them fire, then 0.5 (or 50 per cent) of the neurons have fired. If 75 of the neurons fire, then it is 75 per cent. This gives us a changing value from zero to the maximum.

If 100 per cent of A's neurons fire, that will send the maximum possible output to B (Figure 9). Fewer neurons firing in A means less excitatory activation sent to B. Now, let us say that population A represents visual input that matches an iPhone, while population B represents an iPhone (knowledge of what one is, how they work, etc.) Therefore, the network of Figure 9 represents neural populations capable of recognising an iPhone. Now, imagine seeing a rectangle in the distance where it is not entirely clear what it is. There is some resemblance to an iPhone, but it resembles other rectangular flat things as well. At that point perhaps only 50 per cent of A is firing, but if you notice your phone case on it, 80 per cent of A is firing. Under this interpretation, the amount that A is firing to support the iPhone decision from B changes from a 50 per cent

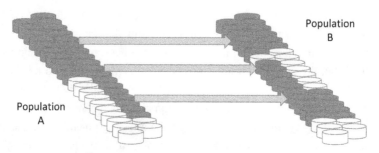

Figure 9 Two populations of neurons A and B. A and B are highly connected such that excitement from A will flow to B. 75 per cent of the neurons in A are firing (non-white in the diagram) to send significant activation to B.

chance of recognising A to an 80 per cent chance (for further discussion, see Spivey, 2008).

The other way to have varying activation is to look at a neuron or neurons over time. A neuron that fires ten times in a second is sending more activation than one that fires five times over a second. Temporal patterns can be more specific than a matter of degree. Firing at a particular point in time or at a certain rate could have a particular meaning. There could also be information in how the neuron's spiking pattern changes over time, rising, falling, and so on. Neural Information Processing is a major field of research, and we will not attempt to survey it (see Liang, Wu, & Gu, 2016). Instead, we are moving towards understanding what neuronal oscillations are. Our next step is to examine techniques for neuroimaging.

One critical tool for studying neural signals over time is EEG (Electro EncephaloGraphy) and the closely related MEG (MagnetoEncephaloGraphy). EEG is done through a grid of sensors placed over the scalp which can measure electrical activity below it. This electric activity is analysed in terms of Event-Related Potentials (ERPs). Potential refers to the resting and action potentials of the neurons. The event part of ERP is some event that the potentials are responding to. For instance, if the neurons are firing in relation to a word being spoken, the word (loosely speaking) is the event, and the firing is the 'potential'. ERPs are often given names like N400 or P300. The N or P refers to Negative or Positive electrical activity. The number refers to the amount of time in milliseconds between the event and the peak electrical activity. So, an N400 would be a peak in negative potential that occurs 400 ms after the event. (For an overview of ERP research in neurolin-guistics, see Segalowitz & Chevalier, 1998.)

Like in acoustic phonetics, you can also perform spectral analysis on the electrical signal from ERP recordings to break the wave into component frequencies. The brain generates waves of activity – oscillations – at repeated, characteristic frequencies. These oscillations have been given Greek letters as names including Delta, Theta, and Gamma from slowest to fastest.[9] The Delta rhythm is the slowest with a range of 1–2 Hz, the Theta in the middle with a period of 4–7 Hz, and the Gamma fastest with a range of 30–50 Hz (Giraud & Poeppel, 2012). Gamma oscillations can also be broken into low and high gamma where high gamma oscillations are faster than low ones.

There seems to be a remarkable correlation between these neuronal oscilla-tions and frequently used speech durations (Figure 10). Converting the Hz to durations, a 50 Hz frequency yields 20 ms periods, a 5 Hz frequency yields

---

[9] Alpha and beta rhythms also exist, but we will focus on the three mentioned. Frustratingly for linguists, the order of slow to fast does not follow the order of the Greek alphabet.

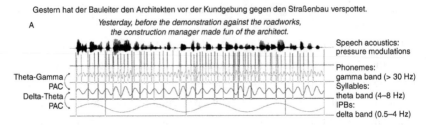

Figure 10 Gamma, Theta, and Delta band oscillations (specified on left) as they correlate with the linguistic unit (right). The fluctuations within each band represent the amplitude envelope of that oscillation. At top is a waveform of the speech. The neuronal oscillations were stimulated by this speech. Reprinted with permission (Meyer, 2018, p. 2610, figure 1).

200 ms periods, and 2 Hz yields 500 ms periods. Within speech, durational patterns that distinguish segments are often close in duration to this 20 ms Gamma range (consider the categorical boundary for Voice Onset Time perception or durations of Formant Transitions); syllables are often around 200 ms in duration on average, matching Theta rhythms; and stress groups (a group of two to three syllables with one syllable stressed) are approximately 500 ms, matching Delta rhythms. The Gamma, Theta, and Delta oscillations match the natural oscillations of speech (Figure 10; Giraud & Poeppel, 2012; Lisman & Jensen, 2013; Luo & Poeppel, 2007).

This cannot be a simple matching process, however. While values such as 200 ms might reflect average durations of syllables, any individual syllable can be significantly shorter, such as when a syllable becomes a single reduced vowel, or longer, such as when a monosyllabic word is spoken in isolation. Syllable durations vary by stress, focus, segmental content, individual speech rate, and more. For neuronal oscillations to match actual speech – and not just averages – they must constantly adjust to the speech as it occurs. Gamma, Theta, and Delta bands all have resting oscillation frequencies. When speech is detected, those existing oscillations adjust to the actual speech of this occasion, modifying their frequencies to match. This can be done by using 'acoustic edges', sudden increases or decreases in the spectral envelope, to continuously adjust the phase of the oscillators. Because of this, speech need not be isochronous, as if it followed a metronome (cf. Turk & Shattuck-Hufnagel, 2013, p. 93). By locking the period and phase of the neuronal oscillations to the period and phase of the amplitude envelope, the brain can 'sample' the incoming signal.

One way to understand the function of such an entrainment is to start by looking at the highest frequency band, the Gamma rhythm. The Gamma rhythm will create a series of short (20 ms in our example) samples of the speech, effectively turning a continuous stream into discrete packages of information. If these samples align with relevant acoustic edges, then it would create packages of relevant speech information to map towards the components of language (segments, gestures, etc.; Giraud & Poeppel, 2012). These packages would have one pattern for periodicity in the signal, another pattern for frication, and so on. This discrete Gamma-based sampling however creates a new problem – tracking the order of these packages. This is where the larger rhythms come into play.

The Theta rhythm comes in periods of approximately 125–250 ms, which are syllable-sized. Entrainment starts with the Theta rhythm as the driver of the oscillator system. Theta follows the phase of the speech signal's amplitude envelope. Both the faster Gamma rhythms and slower Delta rhythms phaselock to Theta (see Figure 10, where arrows on the left show Gamma phase-locked to Theta from above and Delta to Theta from below). The result is that the location of a Gamma sample inside a Theta sample preserves the order of the brief samples. Similarly, Theta rhythms inside Delta rhythms preserve the order of the faster Theta. This use of a hierarchical set of oscillators is very similar to the set of oscillator models in both the OSCAR model of serial order in production and the use of hierarchical oscillators in the AP/TD model.

Theta is considered the primary rhythm because modifying the speech signal to disrupt the Theta rhythm causes disruption to speech comprehension (Luo & Poeppel, 2007). Indeed, we can now explain Ghitza's claim about existing models being incomplete. Ghitza (2011) and Ghitza and Greenberg (2009) produced three types of speech in an experiment. The first was unchanged speech with syllables occurring at a rate of five per second, matching the Theta rhythm and a natural speech rate. The second was a time-compressed speech where syllables occurred at three times that rate, too fast to match an expected Theta. The final type of speech kept that time compression to the speech but added pauses so that the original 5 Hz syllable rate was re-established, matching a viable Theta rhythm again. Participants performed strongly on the unchanged speech and weakly on the time-compressed speech. Most intriguingly, they performed better again when pauses were added into the time-compressed speech. Adding silences into the speech signal (that do not correlate with any speech action like a consonantal closure) improved speech perception. Using sets of stimuli with a range of pauses, participants performed best when the pauses re-established a Theta rhythm and worse when they were shorter or longer than that.

The importance of the Theta oscillation makes sense from a linguistics perspective as well. All languages have syllables. However, a great deal of variation occurs at slower times (higher levels of speech in the spatial metaphor). Stress varies greatly across languages with lexical and phrasal stress.

Stress can be lexically specified, so that it occurs in locations with no synchronic phonological reason, or metrically specified, so that stress falls wherever the metre determines. Some languages do not have stress at all, but those stressless languages may have another unit larger than a syllable, such as an accentual phrase (Jun, 2004). In short, while possibly all languages have one or more prosodic unit(s) larger than a syllable, their forms vary greatly.

All languages have phonological units shorter than a syllable. These could include segments, formant transitions, silences, bursts, and so on, depending on the analysis. However, these short events are too brief to provide evidence for how the events cohere. For example, a formant transition might indicate the place of articulation of a consonant, but we need to know how that place of articulation relates to other acoustic cues to approach meaning.

Syllables, however, are very much about temporal order. The basics of syllable structure – onsets, nuclei, codas – strongly imply temporal order or sequencing, and indeed some slot-filler models use syllabic structure precisely for this ordering. The sonority sequencing hypothesis obviously concerns sequencing. Similarly, phonotactic rules describe where sounds can occur in a sequence: '/ŋ/ cannot be at the start of a syllable' is a statement about allowable sequences, as is one like 'you cannot have two consonants in a sequence at the start of a syllable, etc.'

We have focused so far on neuronal oscillations as a way to sample and keep the order of incoming speech. We have also made one step towards the binding problem: the neuronal oscillations bind the incoming speech because they match the period and phase of that speech. We have also made some steps towards the third limitation of existing phonemic or word recognition models, the attention problem. The Theta, Gamma, and Delta rhythms (as well as Alpha and Beta) are sampling specific acoustic patterns in the speech signal because their periods align. Some research carries this even further.

EEG imaging is a non-invasive technique wherein electrical activity is measured outside the scalp. This brings many insights but does not reveal what representations are being created within the cortex itself. Accessing those requires *intra*cranial measurement where sensors are planted directly on the cortex. This is done primarily with animal models, but animal models are of limited use for a behaviour like language that is unique to humans. However, very rarely, intracranial measurements can be made with humans with full consent. Some clinical treatments of epilepsy require neurosurgery, and some of these participants have consented to more general research during these procedures (Ojemann, 1987).

Fascinating results have emerged from these rare studies, particularly regarding the superior temporal gyrus (STG), one of the most important areas for speech perception.[10] STG is an area that responds to edges in the acoustic signal and vowel onsets (Oganian & Chang, 2019). Theta and Gamma rhythms entrain through using these acoustic edges to set the phase with the speech signal. Pasley and colleagues (2012) showed that it was possible to reconstruct the spectrograms of heard words through monitoring the Gamma oscillations in STG. What was represented in STG depends upon attention. In one set of experiments, the participant listened to either speech from a single voice or speech from a voice with another voice in the background. Only the attended-to voice could be reconstructed via monitoring the STG (Megarini & Chang, 2012; O'Sullivan et al., 2019). In short, neuronal oscillations are one mechanism for attending to speech and carry enough content that the original speech can be reconstructed from them (Lakatos, 2013; Oganian, Fox, and Chang, 2022; Tune & Obleser, 2022).

4.2 Neuronal Oscillations and Developmental Dyslexia

Another promising piece of evidence for the importance of neuronal oscillations in speech perception comes from developmental dyslexia. Dyslexia is a highly varied, controversial phenomenon experienced by 3–10 per cent of the population, in which a person has difficulty reading with no other relevant comorbidities or impairments. The level of reading difficulty can vary, but it can be misleading to think of a person being more or less dyslexic. Instead, dyslexia manifests in varying ways across individuals with some experiencing phonological, visual, rhythmic, or other differences. An additional controversy is whether dyslexia represents a distinct phenomenon or is better understood as a tail of one distribution in reading ability (Elliot, 2020; Fraga González, Karipidis, & Tijms, 2018; Protopas & Parrila, 2018; Wijnants et al., 2012; inter alia).

One account of dyslexia posits that it results from a difference or difficulty in entraining to the neuronal oscillations we have been discussing, typically the slower Theta or Delta oscillations (but also Gamma bands; Cutini, Szűcs, Mead, Huss, & Goswami; 2016; Goswami, 2011; Hämäläinen et al., 2012; Lizarazu et al., 2015). This need not involve reading directly but could be purely through listening to speech. With typical phase-locking, the amplitude of neuronal oscillations would rise and fall with that of the perceived speech, matching speech similar to a spectrogram. However, those with dyslexia demonstrate atypical, less consistent phase-locking for their Theta oscillations to the incoming speech signal. This may be due to a so-called rise-time deficiency

---

[10] The temporal lobe is behind and above your temple, a gyrus is one of the outward folds on the surface of a brain, and *superior* here indicates higher up. In sum, one speech area is a higher up fold above your temple.

(Goswami, 2011). As an example, a primary acoustic difference between a [ba] syllable and a [wa] syllable is the rate at which the increase in amplitude occurs between the consonant and vowel. The rise time is quite sudden for [ba] and slower for [wa]. People with dyslexia can struggle to make this distinction. This has implications beyond distinguishing [b] and [w]: these are examples of acoustic edges, boundaries used for locking the phase of a neuronal oscillator to that of speech. Without successful locking between the Theta band and syllables, an overreliance on Gamma band sampling could result (Goswami, 2011). Giraud and Poeppel (2012) propose that phonological representations would thereby be altered: 'If people with dyslexia parse speech at a frequency slightly higher or lower than the usual low gamma rate, their phonemic representations could exhibit an idiosyncratic format. Phonemic units would be either under-sampled or over-sampled, without necessarily inducing major perceptual deficits' (p. 516). Because the phonological representation is idiosyncratic, when it is used during reading, difficulties emerge.

One limitation to this understanding is the lack of definition of 'idiosyncratic'. Neither Giraud and Poeppel (2012) nor Goswami (2011) pair the proposal with a model of how phonemes might be represented. Indeed, fully symbolic phonemes as we represent them in classic structural phonology should be categorical units of contrast and cannot be idiosyncratic. One way to understand 'idiosyncratic' might be to take inspiration from the XT/3C model.[11] That system included a phoneme-to-acoustics-goal mapping within the phonological component itself. Such a mapping is implicit in the concept that Gamma sampling creates discrete chunks of information for matching to phonemes (though they are likely within different components within XT/3C). If Gamma speech samples are not phase-locked to the speech signal, then what they sample could be extremely noisy. The resulting mapping would include a phoneme connecting to many different acoustic samples.

A one-to-many mapping is not inherently a problem. The whole concept of allophones and sociolinguistic variation indicates that one phoneme could go to many different acoustic realisations. However, if Gamma sampling does not align, phonemes would lack any systematic relationship to the factors known to influence phoneme realisation, including phonetic environment (like an allophone), people (like socio-phonetic variation), physicality (like talking while running or in pain), or conversational situation (background noise, phone vs face-to-face, etc.) Moreover, the noisy samples would include bits generated by other phonemes.

---

[11] XT/3C only models speech production and not speech perception. The current proposal speculates along lines consonant to XT/3C to state how phonological representations could be 'idiosyncratic'.

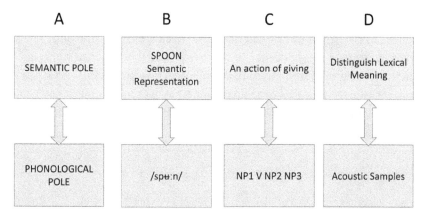

Figure 11 The general form of a construction is presented in (A). (B) represents the morpheme *spoon* with a phonemic phonological pole and a semantic pole; (C) represents a ditransitive syntactic construction with form and meaning; (D) represents treating a 'phoneme' as inherently dipolar as well with a semantics of being able to distinguish morphemes and a phonological pole of its acoustic samples.

Where reading calls on phonological representations, such as in the Dual Route model (Coltheart & Rastle, 1994), that process will be impacted.

One intriguing understanding of this is to reimagine phonemes like constructions in a construction grammar (Goldberg, 2006; Goldberg & Suttle, 2010; Hoffman & Trousdale, 2013). All constructions have a semantic pole and a phonological pole. For example, the construction for a morpheme would have a phonological pole made of a set of phonemes in some order and a semantic pole of its semantic concepts.[12] A syntactic ditransitive construction for English would have an abstract phonological pole representing its form (Noun Phrase1-Verb-Noun Phrase2- Noun Phrase3) and a semantic pole indicating the 'action of giving' meaning of this construction. In the proposal here (Figure 11), the semantic pole of a 'phoneme' represents the primary way that phonemes are explained in classic structural phonology – as mental categories that can distinguish morphemes, the smallest units with meaning. The phonological pole is comprised of the acoustic samples. Critically, the proposal here is that the 'phoneme' is in fact both poles, not only the contrastive semantic side. Just as a lexical construction has both semantics and phonology, the phoneme would have a contrastive component and a qualitative acoustic target component.[13]

---

[12] Different semantic models posit different items to be that semantic pole. Evans (2009) would place the lexical concept, a technical term in its system, as a semantic pole.

[13] This view has some parallels with Natural Phonology as well, wherein phonemes have acoustic or perceptual targets (Donegan & Stampe, 1979; Nathan, 2008).

When reading, it becomes necessary to retrieve phonemes, but since the phonemes are tied to the acoustic samples, which are also tied to other phonemes, it creates a noisy situation in which it is sometimes unclear what phonemes are being 'retrieved'. In sum, in our speculative proposal, phonemes are both acoustic features and contrastive features. Idiosyncratic acoustic sampling then creates noisy, interfering phonemic representations on the acoustic pole.

4.3 Neuronal Oscillators in Serial Recall

We have talked about oscillations in several sections now:

- as the context signal that places items in serial order (OSCAR)
- as a timing mechanism for gesture scores (AP/TD)
- as an ordering and binding mechanism between acoustics and neural processing
- as a source of differing language representations and behaviour.

This raises a logical question: is there any connection between all these oscillations? We will turn next to one proposal that indeed builds a connection between neuronal oscillations for speech perception and serial order.

Hartley, Hurlstone, and Hitch (2016) raise an issue with serial recall models such as OSCAR: those models do not explain where the context signal comes from. Most serial recall models, including OSCAR, stipulate what the signal is and modify that signal to more closely approximate experimental results on speakers' serial recall behaviour, but the context signal is entirely stipulated. The success of the model provides evidence for it, but the signal is not modelling any known neural mechanism. Hartley and colleagues propose a modification to OSCAR where the oscillator-based context signal arises from the stimulus itself. They term this new model the bottom-up multi-scale population oscillator or BUMP model. In this model, oscillators are used but, paralleling the speech perception literature we have just reviewed, the oscillators are built from the oscillations of the signal. BUMP postulates neural populations that oscillate at varying rates that are attuned to the incoming speech signal. When the signal's amplitude envelope oscillates at a rate similar to the rate of the neural population, the neurons will become highly active, entraining to the phase and periods of the signal. These neural populations resonate with the quasi-periodic components of the speech envelope and form the context signal in an OSCAR-like way.

While neuronal oscillations that reflect oscillations in the speech envelope make us think of Gamma, Theta, and Delta oscillations, the BUMP model does not implement those oscillations directly. Rather, they implemented a series of fifteen log-spaced frequencies to constitute the context signal. If the signal's envelope included Gamma, Theta, and Delta oscillations, then the neural populations of BUMP would echo that; however, those particular ranges are not in the oscillation designs themselves.

The rest of the model operates in similar ways to OSCAR. During learning, the item and signal-derived context signal are stored as a combined unit. Upon retrieval, the context signal is replayed and the item that most closely matches the combination of context and item is retrieved. Items are then activated through a competitive queuing mechanism. The primary innovation of the BUMP model then, over not just OSCAR but most context signal models, is basing the context on the speech stimulus itself. Speech provides sufficient patterning for maintaining serial order without researchers having to design a separate context signal.

This has unifying potential. The BUMP mechanism could be 'a starting point for a more general theory of serial order in language processing, potentially linking speech perception, speech production and verbal short-term memory through their common dependence on rhythm and timing' (Hartley et al., 2016, p. 136). The BUMP model can also help us understand the connection to dyslexia as well. If we use the speech envelope itself to coordinate serial order of speech production and perception in a loop, then we should expect serial order problems if the speech envelope is harmed or differing. With BUMP, we might not need construction-like phonemes with an acoustic pole. Instead, we need to understand how the atypical perception of the signal interferes with serial order during perception and production.

4.4 Interim Summary

In our selected tour of dynamic approaches to phonological processing, we have made substantial progress in understanding speech production and perception. However, in a sense, this is low-hanging fruit for dynamic approaches to language. Producing and perceiving speech are the places where time is most obvious. Linguistic acoustics has been measuring durations for decades. To speak and comprehend, it is clear that we must keep things in the right order. To produce or perceive short versus long vowels, we clearly need to care about durations. However, other parts of language are traditionally seen as primarily structural. 'Higher language' is presented with groups, trees, constituents, and such, and no longer talks much about durations. As we have mentioned, phonological rules commonly utilise phonemes in the right order or specify a sound being between other sounds without indicating how this is accomplished. This Element opened by asking whether a dynamic focus on language would change how we think about language even structurally. Has it?

In fact, our examination of time in speech has raised concepts for structural language already. For instance, in the XT/3C model, which explicitly preserves phonemes, its phonological component contains a mapping between phonemes and acoustic features. We also suggested that a phoneme might be viewed as a construction, with the contrastive function of phonemes analogous to the semantic pole and the acoustic features from Gamma, Theta, and Delta oscillations as their phonological pole. Finally, articulatory phonology, motivated by several questions of language dynamics, explicitly changes not just what phonemes and allophones are but the phonological representation of words and allophonic processes. Therefore, these approaches are suggesting significant changes to structural phonological theory.

Despite these tantalising ideas, there are many common phonological questions that have no clear answer in the paradigms suggested. These include:

1. How do stress and weight systems work?
2. How does phonological development occur?
3. How do we account for non-local phonology like vowel harmonies?

If our dynamic theories cannot comment on phonological questions like these, perhaps this work on speech production and speech perception is 'downstream' from structural linguistics. Some comprehensiveness is needed before we take the ideas too seriously as alternatives to classic structural phonology.

To tackle questions like these, we turn now to one more major theory.

5 Dynamic Intention Selection and Coordination

'Dynamic intention selection and coordination' (DISC) is a term I am introducing here to refer to dynamic approaches primarily developed by Sam Tilsen of Cornell University, along with related work in dynamic systems and phonology (Tilsen, 2016, 2018, 2019c; inter alia). Tilsen uses the term 'selection-coordination theory' (Tilsen, 2019a) for his own work and considers it an extension of AP/TD. Indeed, DISC keeps the gestural score as a key component of phonology. Therefore, it's a phonology without phonemes based around gestures; however, DISC adds a rich, and different, set of control mechanisms (Tilsen, 2018) that modify the theory in significant ways. One novel concept is the neural **dynamic field**, hence the here-introduced name 'dynamic intention selection and coordination' (Gafos & Kirov, 2009; Harper, 2021; Roon & Gafos, 2016; Schöner & Spencer, 2015; Tilsen, 2018, 2020).[14]

---

[14] Tilsen did not originate dynamic field theory, which this list of citations and the explication to come should make clear. However, I have said DISC primarily surveys Tilsen's work, because Tilsen's theory including dynamic fields is the most comprehensive presentation.

To understand dynamic fields, let us revisit gestural scores from articulatory phonology. A score represents time intervals of gestural activation, and each gesture is associated with a target value for a particular tract variable. When the gesture is active, the corresponding tract variable evolves towards that target. However, how are these values generated and maintained? We need a mechanism that can (1) take diverse inputs because a speaker's articulation changes over circumstances and time, (2) store a pattern over time representing the speaker's idiolect, and (3) generate a sustained target value despite all of the inputs while also allowing variation. Dynamic field theory can be used to do this (Roon & Gafos, 2016). Dynamic fields were created in the study of motor control systems (Erlhagen & Schöner, 2002; Schöner & Spencer, 2016). In this context, the dynamic field is a spatially organised population of neurons changing over time. One goal is to model diverse inputs producing a single coherent output, which the field accomplishes by producing a sustained peak activation from many input activations. The field implements this through its physical structure where neurons excite neurons nearby and inhibit neurons further away.

Take neurons A–E near one another and V–Z further away (Figure 12). When activation comes to A, it will send excitation to B–E while inhibiting V–Z. Similarly, if activation comes to B, it will excite its neighbours while inhibiting

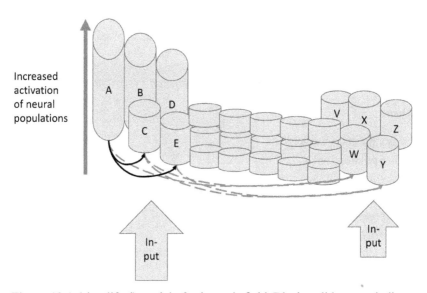

Figure 12 A (simplified) model of a dynamic field. Black, solid arrows indicate self- and neighbour-excitation, while red, dashed arrows indicate distal-inhibition. The large arrows represent some input to the field. Because A–E are receiving more input (bigger input arrow), they are able to win the competition and suppress V–Z even though V–Z receive some input (smaller input arrow).

V–Z. This process is similar to competitive queuing in that each area is competing to win by activating itself and inhibiting its competition. The winner will be the area receiving the most input activation, resulting in a single peak in the field despite multiple conflicting inputs. Like the dynamic competitive queuing, dynamic fields incorporate a threshold that counts as being selected. Because an area's activation is self-sustaining (neighbours continue to excite neighbours), it can sustain an 'on' state (Harper, 2021; Roon & Gafos, 2016). The field integrates multiple sources of information and turn that into something stable. For instance, information such as seeing the letter *p* and information such as thinking of the word *petunia* might both contribute towards activating a /p/ related value in the field. Therefore, multiple inputs are transformed into one energetic peak.

A dynamic field is organised spatially where areas of the field correspond to target values for a tract variable. As an approximation, one area would represent 'dental', another 'alveolar' and a third 'post-alveolar'. However, in the work of Harper (2021), targets are not categorical like this, but instead a continuous range of values. Each dynamic field represents a different tract parameter, so one field would consider tongue tip location, another tongue tip closure, a third lip aperture closure, and so on. Peaks on the dynamic fields create precise articulatory targets for that person. A tract variable takes on a form when its target values are specified, and these fields generate target values through a dynamic process.

The field is governed by a differential equation that evolves over time (from Harper, 2021, eq 4.1):

$$\tau dA(x,t) = -A(x,t) + h + input(x,t) + interaction\ (x,t) + noise. \qquad \text{(Eq.1)}$$

Where:

- x is a point on the field
- t is a point in time t
- *A(x,t)* represent the activation of x at time t
- τ is the rate of decay in activation
- h represents a resting level for point x
- *input(x,t)* represents all inputs to x at time t
- *interaction(x,t)* represents the excitatory and inhibitory connections towards x at time t
- *noise* represents noisy activation to x.

Putting them all together, the activation at some point on the field is a sum of the activation from previous time steps (*A*), a resting activation level (*h*), input activation, and interaction from other parts of the field. When there is no input, triggering no interaction, the resting level h determines activation. In the terms of dynamic systems theory, it therefore acts as a **fixed-point attractor**. When all other sources of activation are removed, h represents the point the system will return to. Note that h does not change over short timeframes, while input and interaction do.

Input (x,t) is an umbrella term to represent all inputs to the system. It comes in two types: (1) task input and (2) specific input (Harper, 2021, p. 153). The **task input** component is a distribution over the possible levels this variable can take, called its **preshape**. Like an electromagnetic field that has some value at all points in space, the dynamic field also maintains some activation level at all points on the field. The preshape gives the resting levels of the field. With the right input, any possible point in the field might be selected as the tract variable target; however, the preshape builds in activation at certain places, making them more likely to be selected. The preshape's distribution will take on different values based upon experience. If a speaker's most likely location for a tongue tip gesture is slightly forward (or back or anywhere), that is represented in the preshape. Informally, the preshape represents the rut that a speaker most easily falls into when activating this gesture.

Within this system, the activation level is thresholded. It is only when the threshold is passed that the gesture is selected. This allows the field to sustain a single choice, rather than sending a continuous distribution of choices (differing activation levels) to connected systems. The preshape increases the activation in one area of the field, making it closer to the activation threshold so that it is more likely to win the competitive race, all things being equal. A threshold for selection with a dynamic field resembles the activation threshold within selection for competitive queuing.

The **specific input** component to the dynamic field refers to all other non-task inputs. 'This input can come from an external source, such as a heard speech sound or a read word, or it can come from an internal impulse such as the decision to say a certain word' (Harper, 2021, p. 156). This dynamic planning field therefore operates as a hub in the production network. An intention to utter a word would be an input to the planning field, as is what is perceived or read. This could also include socio-phonetic factors such as identity, speaker relationships, aspirations, and so on (Foulkes & Doherty, 2006). Indeed, Harper's research project is not to model one standard pronunciation for a language or speaker community, but in fact the variation and idiolects of individuals. This is accomplished by varying the tract and specific input distributions.

Tilsen terms these dynamic fields applied to speech production **intentional planning fields** (Tilsen, 2019b, 2018), the term I will use hence. The behaviour of the field depends upon its spatial structure and pattern of connections. The previously mentioned planning fields generate a single peak to yield a single active target value. A different spatial structure of the field creates different phonological patterns. Tilsen's (2019b) article 'Space and time in models of speech rhythm' demonstrates how the spatial structure of dynamic fields can change their behaviour to produce quite different patterns. It brings up structural descriptions of stress assignment and metrical phonology, where stress is assigned to prosodic units moving directionally from a left or right edge (e.g., Hayes, 1995).

> The spatial vocabulary (i.e., left, right, and edge) is somewhat odd, because words do not really have edges, and because the mapping of left/right to earlier/ later is arbitrary. To say that words have 'edges' relies on a metaphor in which time is a linear space and syllables are objects arranged in that space. (Tilsen, 2019b, p. 41)

However, if words are not blocks in space, but dynamic forces or actions in time, then they can overlap in ways physical objects cannot. Also, time is inherently directional, proceeding from cause to effect. Events should only move forward in time and 'left' and 'right' are arbitrary definitions. Yet, stress assignment is not asymmetric like time and does appear to make assignment in a specific direction. English, for instance, assigns stress in trochaic patterns starting from the right edge of a word. (For example, Mississippi becomes | ˌmɔ. sɔ | ˈsɔ.pi |, with stress on the first syllable of each metrical foot.) Tilsen argues there is in fact a spatial dimension that gives left, right, and edge meaning – within a dynamic field, termed a **motor sequencing field**.

Tilsen proposes a set of dynamic fields with different spatial structures to perform online stress assignment. These fields constitute the components that, when combined, create the prosodic patterns we find in the world. The first is an intentional planning field with singular, stable points that drives articulatory tract variables such as tongue location and closure. The second field, the motor sequencing field, creates a structure of standing waves of neural activation (Figure 13a and 13b). This pattern is formed by the excitatory and inhibitory connections between neurons. These connections create blocks of neural subpopulations that can generate a wave pattern: oscillating high and low activation.[15] An additional field creates a wave of activation with a simple peak of high activation that either rapidly declines from the peak or rapidly increases to the peak (Figure 13c).

When this activation peak and the oscillating wave of the motor sequencing field are combined, the result is an oscillation with one point higher than the other points in the wave (Figure 13d). This creates a wave of secondary stress with primary stress occurring on either side of the wave. This oscillating pattern

---

[15] Goldstein and Iskarous (2018) build a related model for generating prosodic patterns via dynamic fields.

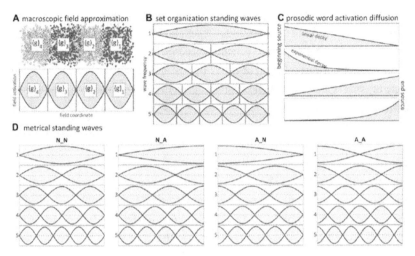

Figure 13 The components of Tilsen's (2019b, p. 58, figure 6) wave/field model of prosodic patterns. Top-left (a) shows how structured neural populations can produce a standing wave. Top-centre (b) displays standing waves of varying syllable counts. Top-right (c) creates another wave with a peak for prosodic words. Bottom (d) presents different combinations of (b) and (c) to produce common prosodic patterns in the world's languages. Reprinted with permission.

then couples with the dynamic shape of the gestural intentional planning field so that peaks in activation in the prosodic field affect activation in the gestural intentional planning field. The high prosodic points provide additional, patterned energy to the gestural system.

In this way, a dynamic system of fluctuating fields, connectivity, and energy levels can specify prosodic patterns found in the world's languages.[16] However, a gap remains in the theory as we have explained it so far: prosodic patterns affect prosodic units like mora or syllables, but gestural scores do not have mora or syllables to activate; there are only coordinated articulatory gestures. Tilsen addresses this with an additional change to the mechanisms which control gestures. Pure AP/TD uses coupled oscillators for timing of gestures. Tilsen (2013, 2014, 2016) argues this is insufficient. We will look at two lines of argument.

The first line of argument comes from motor control generally. Muscle movements do not start with carefully timed coordination. Expert practice demonstrates precisely timed coordination, but not beginner practice. A beginning piano player plays each key one by one, making sure each finger goes to the target

---

[16] This explication simplifies Tilsen's (2019b) full proposal, which must be read before evaluation can occur.

location. Despite this, mistakes occur. As expertise increases, what was a sequential selection of keys becomes a set chord that they can play as a unit on command. Separately timed sequences become highly coordinated arpeggios. The difference between playing keys one by one and playing a chord or arpeggio is one of control and timing. The chord is selected to play an entire group at one moment. Key-by-key playing is selecting one key, then the next key, then the next.

The same process occurs with typing, where beginners laboriously plan out sequences of button presses, while experts can coordinate common sequences with speed (Logan, 2018). You can tell that you are selecting common groupings when you accidentally type one word for another. For example, I frequently type *not* for *now* even though the *t* and *w* keys are not adjacent. *Not* is a sequence I produce frequently and sometimes I choose it erroneously. Similarly, I find myself typing *ration* for *ratio* frequently. The *-tion* sequence is common in English, while *-tio* with no *n* is rare.

Tilsen's proposal then is that, in early speech development, children primarily use a serial order mechanism for **selection** and subsequently move to a faster mechanism for **coordination**. Serial order selection involves initiating one movement, waiting for feedback that its target has been achieved, and then suppressing it to initiate the next. Coordination allows activation of multiple actions at once. Speakers will develop from sequentially controlled speech to coordinated speech, from single selected actions to multiple coordinated actions. This will change due to increasing expertise using internal feedback versus external feedback (see an explanation of the difference below), but also due to experience with community languages. Communities of speakers might coordinate some phonetic relationships and keep other relationships selected, with differing communities making differing choices. Since selection and coordination involve two different timing mechanisms, the result would be different prosodic patterns.

A second line of argument against AP/TD's oscillator-based coordination as the exclusive timing mechanism comes from the need to choose what to coordinate. If certain items are going to be coordinated in time, then the items to coordinate must be selected. Gestures with coordination are phonological representations of lexical items; they must be learned or created. For conventional words in a language, they would be acquired over time. For words that are made up in the moment of conversation, they need to be generated on the fly. Lexical creativity requires that we *select* gesture combinations that we may not have selected before.

In short, to account for timing patterns, particularly over development, Tilsen proposes that we need both a selection mechanism and a coordination mechanism. For coordination, Tilsen retains oscillators. For selection, Tilsen (2014, 2016, 2018) uses competitive queuing, which we saw above as a common mechanism to implement serial order. The gesture with the highest activation is selected. It is then suppressed, allowing for the item with the next highest activation to be selected.

In our earlier discussion of competitive queuing, we did not specify *how* an item is suppressed once it passes the threshold for selection. One possibility is that monitoring the results of selection is used to suppress. The speaker selects X. They then monitor sensory feedback to determine that X was in fact produced. Based upon this feedback, they suppress X's selection, allowing the next item to be selected. If an item is not suppressed, it could continue to be re-selected. Within speech, this will involve monitoring the success of producing some phonological target, such as a phoneme, syllable, or gesture. This explanation of monitoring provides an intuitive understanding – did we do what we were supposed to do? If so, then mark the action successful – but taken literally it introduces problems. It suggests conscious monitoring, which is rare, and suggests that something 'knows' what is supposed to happen. A more accurate understanding can be seen in Figure 14, representing a **forward model** approach to monitoring (based on Pickering & Clark, 2014; Pickering & Garrod, 2013, 2014; Wolpert, 1997; see also Tilsen, 2016).

The fundamental notion is to put prediction at the heart of things (Clark, 2013, 2015). When an action is selected, it is sent in two directions. One

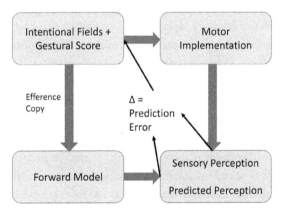

Figure 14 A forward model of speech articulation and planning. A gestural score drives the motor plant to articulate speech and sends an efference copy to a forward model. This forward model predicts the sensory results. The difference between sensory perception and predicted perception is the prediction error, which can then affect the commands from the gestural score.

direction will be towards the actual implementation through motor control. The other direction is to predict the sensory consequences of what will happen. This occurs through sending an efference copy to a so-called forward model that takes the action and predicts, based upon experience, what the results will be. The prediction and the result can then be compared (Figure 14). If the results meet expectations, then the selected item can be suppressed. However, if not, then some sort of repair might occur, such as re-selecting the intended item or suppressing the item and selecting another. An expert system would have minimal prediction error, where what they do matches their predictions of what they do.

Pickering and Garrod (2014) express this in terms of intentions. We intend to perform an action and seek feedback about the success of our intentions. We can map this back to the DISC system. The intentional planning field takes input from multiple sources, including the intention to speak a certain word from a semantic system. These sources of activation create a peak of activation at one point on the dynamic field, generating an 'On' state. The location on the field's 'On' state specifies the value for tract variables within a gestural score. The peaks of activation from the different planning fields are the activating agent for the competitive queuing mechanism so that items are selected. These selections both drive the gesture motor system and generate an efference copy for the forward model. The forward model predicts the acoustic/auditory results of the selection. The prediction and actuality are then compared. If the error is small – perhaps under some threshold – then the selection was successful, and it will be suppressed.

Feedback based on sensory input requires an extensive process of intention, selection, motor output, sensory perception, and error comparison. This **external feedback** yields slow suppression and therefore action. The next action cannot be selected until you have seen the success of the first through the senses. However, a faster source of feedback can develop: **internal feedback**. In this case, the results of the forward model itself can be used for suppression. If the outcome is predicted, we utilise that immediately for suppression. A risk with internalisation of feedback is increased error; a prediction may be incorrect. A major benefit is speed, as internal feedback becomes available faster than external. This all implies a developmental pattern from selection with external feedback to selection with internal feedback to coordination (Tilsen, 2016).

In the early stages of phonological development, most speech gestures are ordered through a competitive queuing selection mechanism, one selection at a time. As the child develops their phonological knowledge and motor skill, they learn to **co-select** gestures to be triggered at once. Part of phonological knowledge is awareness that some target sounds cannot be produced with singular gestures sequentially. Many sounds require multiple gestures with precise timing. Producing voiced and voiceless bilabial stops requires co-selecting both a lip gesture and a glottal gesture. The **co-selection set** determines what can be coordinated via oscillators. Coordination allows highly precise timing that is impossible through competitive queuing because queuing requires activation and suppression via external feedback before activating the next item. Voice onset times, which must be controlled to a level of tens of milliseconds, require coordination. To produce them, the consonantal and vowel gestures are co-selected, {CV}, and coordinated so that the vocal tract can produce the right timing before any feedback, external or internal, arrives. Languages will offer different requirements for co-selection. If a language never contrasts voiced and voiceless stops, then the child may never co-select the oral and glottal gestures, while they would co-select them in a language that does contrast the two.

The co-selection set is a powerful phonological idea. There has been a debate for decades about the validity of phonemes (for recent examples, see Boucher, 2021, Fowler et al., 2016). Turk and Shattuck-Hufnagel (2020) devote an extensive literature review towards arguing for their presence. This contrasts with AP/TD, which does away with the phoneme and generates phonological patterns with gestures and gestural scores. Other basic units, such as the phonological feature or the syllable, have also been proposed. A co-selection set of multiple gestures can generate units of differing sizes that – in particular circumstances and for particular communities – act like phonemes, mora, syllables, and so on. Indeed, many traditional units of linguistic structure simply can be viewed as approximations of co-selection sets. Co-selection sets are not identical to symbolic phonemes or syllables. The co-selection sets select temporal forces to create articulatory gestures.

Returning to the prosodic dynamic fields, we can now say that they would bind with co-selection sets. One 'counts' co-selection sets left and right for stress assignment. Additionally, having both selection and coordination moves towards an account of prosodic weight (i.e., syllables being heavy or light), or having mora. All gestures begin as separate selections: {C}{V}{C}. Many languages require precise timing relations between pre-vocalic consonantal gestures and vocalic gestures, which necessitates a move towards coordinated control within a single co-selection set: {CV}. As the onset and nucleus gestures are co-selected, they are only one 'mora'. It is rare for an onset alone to have weight, because coordination requirements of CV syllables usually require co-selection of gestures. This leaves postvocalic coda consonants as a separate co-selection set and thus acting like a separate mora: {CV}{C}. The syllable consists of two co-selection sets or two mora where a coda consonant has weight like the vocalic gestures. Other languages might, however, bring some coda gestures within the same co-selection set as the vocalic gestures, {CVC}, so that those codas do not give weight.

Finally, combining the intentional planning field with selection and coordination methods of control generates non-local phonological patterns, such as harmony patterns, that AP/TD struggles with. In DISC, selection is managed by competitive queuing where the order is determined by the relative activation levels of each item. The intentional planning field drives those activation levels determining the subsequent order. Thus, it acts like the context signal in the serial recall models.

Activation in the intentional planning field itself, before a thresholded selection is passed, can result in anticipatory posturing before a gesture is fully activated (Tilsen, 2020). Additionally, the interaction of each component can generate seemingly non-local phonological patterns (Tilsen, 2019a). If a gesture gets activated but it does not get suppressed for an extended period, the gesture could influence subsequent gestures as long as they do not directly contradict it. This will not work for patterns such as certain consonant harmonies that appear to 'skip' intervening consonants. Consider a word such as /ba.sa.na/ being pronounced as [masana]. Within DISC, these sorts of patterns can result from the interaction of intentional planning and selection. To produce an /n/, the intentional field boosts an open velar gesture that produces nasality. If the intentional field boosts the velar gesture early, anticipatory posturing or limited nasality could occur through activating the open velar gesture on the /b/. Some languages might have such anticipations but never phonologise it, leaving it as a hard-to-detect, sporadic phonetic pattern. Other language communities, however, might phonologise the pattern. Hearers re-analyse the early activation as intentional activation and change it so that it becomes the intended pattern.

With this extended discussion of planning fields, selection, gestures, and so on, it might seem like we've forgotten that this Element is about time in phonological processing. However, we have not erred. The time dimension has been critical throughout in a number of ways:

1. The DISC model contains both competitive queuing, which is a theory of serial order, and oscillator-based coordination, which is specified in terms of periods and phases in time.
2. Much of the theoretical development is motivated by a desire to explain the dynamic patterns of language and the explanations are also written in dynamic terms. The full theory is treated and formalised as dynamic systems.
3. In DISC, all of the critical items are about forces in time. Gestural scores represent periods in time in which a force can activate the motor system.

The dynamic intentional planning fields are also temporal patterns of activation influencing gestural systems.

4. Phonological patterns are not rules or constraints but temporal patterns of activation, suppression, and control over time.

6 Gathering Key Ideas

It is time to take the ideas we have reviewed throughout this Element and see what they can tell us about speech and phonology.

One key idea used repeatedly was that of dynamic oscillators. In almost every section of this Element (with the notable exception of XT/3C), we have seen the proposal of oscillators as a key mechanism. A set of oscillators was proposed to provide the learning context for serial learning and recall in the OSCAR models for speech production. AP/TD utilised them to coordinate gestures. Oscillations appeared again in speech perception used for serial ordering, controlling attention, and speech sampling. Differences in oscillator tracking were also posited as an account of dyslexia. In the DISC model, those oscillators persisted, though they were restricted towards coordination of a limited set of gestures (within the co-selection set) rather than as the general mechanism. This naturally raises the question: why? Why do so many theorists keep turning to oscillators in their attempts to understand (timing in) language?

One reason is that rhythmic behaviour is certainly a timekeeping tool that people do use. It shows up most clearly in music where highly synchronised actions can occur by becoming entrained with a beat. A group of highly trained musicians can perform actions – singing, a pluck of a string, a beat of a drum, and so on – with incredible temporal precision. This coordination ability can extend out to tens of thousands of people at the largest events, such as a concert. In a major broadcast of a musical performance, millions of people across the globe could be synchronised through rhythm.

It is *possible* for people to produce language with a beat. In a chorus, dozens of people produce language to a beat. We can sing and produce poetry rhythmically. Moving towards natural conversational speech, things become less clear. While linguists often speak of languages being mora-timed, syllable-timed, or stress-timed, the basis of this is not clear (Arvaniti, 2009; Grabe & Low, 2002; Lehiste, 1977; Ramus, Nespor, & Mehler, 1999; White & Mattys, 2007). Often the term quasi-periodic is used to indicate periodic structure that is not truly isochronous.

One solution to varying rhythm in speech is to argue that timing for natural speech is not periodic and oscillator-based, but it might be made periodic in special circumstances. This is a two-mechanism solution. Turk and Shattuck-Hufnagel (2020) explicitly removed oscillators from their XT/3C theory of speech production. They allow that in singing or chant, language might be made periodic, but that was not the primary timing mechanism of natural speech.

Another approach is to have a single mechanism that can be more periodic in some situations (like singing to a beat) and less periodic in others (like natural speech). Essentially, competing goals with different weights can drive speech toward and away from periodicity even when one periodic mechanism exists. Reduced periodicity for natural speech comes from the other constraints on speech beyond rhythm, including consonants and vowels of differing duration, morphosyntactic constraints, and the extemporaneous nature of conversation. In normal conversation, these constraints disguise the pressure of an oscillating timing mechanism. However, sometimes we do give more weight to this periodicity, changing gestural durations and content to match the desired period. This approach says that periodicity is always a driver of action, but it can have more or less sway, depending on the speech goals.

Musical rhythm is not the only reason for the borrowing of oscillators into linguistic theory. Oscillation is well understood as a timing mechanism. We understand beats and sub-divisions of beats, with music psychology being an entire field. We know that rhythm can guide attention to certain points in time (Jones, 1976; Jones, 1986; Large & Jones, 1999). Mechanical clocks, our primary timekeeping tools, are oscillators. Even atomic clocks are based on the oscillations of a caesium atom. Oscillation also has a robust mathematical theory that's centuries old. Trigonometry's roots go back hundreds of years, and some aspects go back thousands. Therefore, there is a clear formal description sitting there waiting for use. Also, as reviewed throughout this Element, we know that neural populations in fact oscillate. EEG/MEG imaging measures neuronal oscillations, and we are making progress in understanding their neural implementation. In sum, oscillators provide a mechanism that must connect to language in some capacity, has a formal description for modelling, has a neural instantiation, and is clearly connected to time.

Looking at speech as an approximation to music, where it is periodic if it is more like music and less periodic if it is not, might miss a source of the speech signal's periodic behaviour, however. Segmental speech, be it with gestural scores or phone sequences, oscillates between closing and opening gestures. These closures and openings might be highly regular in time or not due to items like consonant clusters, but the opening and closing is continual and universal. The series of constrictions and openings will result in oscillations in the acoustic envelope. Even a serial order mechanism like competitive queuing is periodic. Competitive queuing operates by selecting an item for production and then suppressing it. If it queues a sequence of items (which it will typically do since this is *serial* order), then that implies an oscillation between activation and suppression repeatedly.[17]

Regardless, many questions regarding oscillations remain. The gap between what we know about oscillations and concepts of structural linguistics is large (Haegens & Golumbic, 2018; Protopas, 2014) with many remaining questions (Boucher, Gilbert, & Jemel, 2019; Tune & Obleser, 2022). Moreover, we have reasons to question oscillation as the exclusive timing measure. Turk and Shattuck-Hufnagel (2020) raises concerns that oscillator-based systems drive the *initiation* of motions when it is often the *endpoints* that are the primary targets (among other criticisms). It might be possible to modify oscillators to target endpoints but there are significant challenges to doing so. Regardless, it is unlikely that oscillators are the only mechanism utilised to control timing in speech. (See Section 5.)

To see what is available beyond oscillators, let us collect ideas presented through this text and look for recurring concepts.

1. The serial recall models, XT/3C, and DISC all require some system of selecting what to utter. This suggests we need **items** to select and a **selection** process.
2. One successful model to select and maintain an order is competitive queuing. For competitive queuing to operate, it requires both an **activation** agent to initiate activation levels for queuing and a **suppression** agent to halt an item selected.
3. One plausible suppression mechanism is **feedback**. This feedback could be external, where the senses are used to detect success, or internal, where a prediction of success can suppress the selection.
4. Feedback operates through an **error** comparison of intention and results. This error comparison partially resembles general tau theory that uses a comparison between current state and goal state to drive action.
5. While items must be selected, the selection and suppression loop is too slow for some actions. In these cases, items must be **co-selected** and **coordinated** in time with oscillators as a viable mechanism. Any timing requirements faster than selection allows requires some other timing mechanism, such as oscillator-based coordination or general tau theory.
6. Our models differ about their starting point, but any speech production model requires **motor control** near the end. For speech, the vocal tract must produce precisely timed motion.

---

[17] Periodicity in speech remains a contested issue (for a good discussion, see Turk & Shattuck-Hufnagel, 2013).

7. The use of perceptive feedback in speech production requires that speech
   gestures are recoverable from the speech signal (Iskarous, 2016), else the
   system would not know what to suppress. There is a speech production/
   speech perception loop.

6.1 The Speech Perception/Speech Production Loop

A complicated series of connections between speech production and perception
must exist. This has been examined for decades in many ways, such as the
analysis-by-synthesis approach (Stevens & Halle, 1967), and we will not review
it all. Instead, the focus is simply on what issues this Element has raised.
Monitoring as part of production requires that either internal or external feedback is 'checked' with every single selection. The timing of the perception/
production loops becomes critical as well. Only speech that arrives with
a certain time delay can be external feedback (Sasisekaran, 2012). Perceived
speech must arrive after production, or it cannot be the speech from the speaker.
Speech heard seconds after production cannot possibly be what the speaker just
uttered, nor can speech heard before articulators can move. Internal feedback
will have its own timing delay, shorter than external feedback. And speech that
arrives before production is not used for suppression at all but might actually
excite speech. Phonetic alignment wherein we produce sounds more like what
we perceive indicates a positive link from perception to production. This can
occur over years such as between caregivers and children (St Pierre, Cooper, &
Johnson, 2021) or within a single conversation (Ostrand & Chodroff, 2021;
Pickering & Garrod, 2004). Over time, a developing speaker comes to echo
their community in speech patterns as well, which is why a community can have
an accent.

Moreover, we saw with the BUMP model that production can be driven by
the speech signal itself as the context signal. Could we integrate BUMP and
DISC such that DISC's production model uses the speech signal to drive
speech? More generally, does the BUMP model tell us anything about production of speech outside the confines of a serial recall experiment? We need to
consider the differences between serial recall and conversation more fully.

There are some similarities between the two. In a serial recall task, the
participant hears speech and then repeats that speech. In a natural conversation,
a speaker hears their conversation partner utter a speech string and utters
a speech string in return. Both situations require methods of learning sequences
and producing them. However, the response in a natural conversation is not the
same as in serial recall. A conversational response is rarely a full repetition.
Conversational alignment can occur where both speakers partially mimic the

semantics, syntax, lexicon, and phonetics of each other (Pickering & Garrod, 2004). However, each speaker also makes novel contributions, which is what pushes the conversation forward (Fusaroli & Tylén, 2016; Mills, 2014).

These differences imply that the 'context signal' for conversation will be quite different from that of a serial recall task. In the BUMP model, the context signal is entirely reliant on what was heard before. The speaker has no goal other than repeating what was just heard, and so the items recalled are those that most closely match the combination of items and context signal. In a conversation, the context signal that drives speech will need to be dynamically created from multiple systems so that items never mentioned in the conversation can be retrieved and used in a conversationally relevant way. We cannot directly take the BUMP model and use heard speech to guide selection of produced speech. At a minimum, there is a timing problem. A speech signal cannot drive or initiate the very speech that created it.

However, this does not mean that a speech signal has no relationship to speech intentions and planning. Harper's (2021) inputs to the dynamic planning field require a link between what we hear and how we speak. Perceptual input can shift the precise articulatory goals produced by the dynamic field. Doing this could necessitate translating what has been heard into terms equivalent to placement on an articulatory planning field. For perceptual input to shift the value for a tract variable, what is heard must also supply a Tongue Tip value. If so, we must be able to 'hear speech gestures'. This is reminiscent of the motor theory of speech perception (Galantucci, Fowler & Turvey, 2006; Liberman & Mattingly, 1985, but for such a loop without assuming the motor theory, see also Monahan et al., 2022; Stevens, 2002). What we hear influencing what we produce does not require a strong version of the thesis where only speech gestures are heard, nor that words can only be recognised via their gestures. However, it does require that gestures are recovered by most speakers.[18]

There are then some overlaps between XT/3C and DISC in that both require connecting acoustic values with phonemic representations. In XT/3C, qualitative acoustic targets map with phonemes (embedded in prosodic contexts); in DISC, as represented by Harper (2021), quantitative acoustic samples map with quantitative intentional planning values. While the latter mapping is a continuing research question, we can see potential by blending gestural scores and intentional field activation levels into an updated visualisation. The gestural score shows periods of gestural activity over time, which become intentional field activations over time. To visualise, we can utilise concepts from the

---

[18] This Element has generally assumed someone using a spoken language with hearing. This need not be the only way that language works.

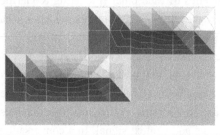
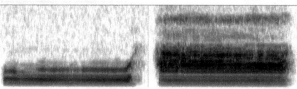

Figure 15 Activation levels for tract variable values over time are represented
on the Taskogram (bottom-left) and a spectrogram for [u] and [ɐ] (top-right).
The spectrogram follows the Taskogram with some time lag because the
intention to produce takes some time to realise and perceive.

spectrogram. We place time on the X-axis, tract values on the Y, and activation
levels on the Z, with darker colouring indicating more energy. Figure 15 shows
an actual spectrogram for [u] and [ɐ] vowels on the bottom right and a mock
'Taskogram' on the top-left, mapping production values and acoustic values
into a similar schematic. Learned connections between the two could generate
a translation. Exploring such mappings between the Taskogram and spectrogram could be fruitful.

7 Approaching a Dynamic Model of Speech and Phonology

To assess the contribution of dynamic approaches to phonology, we can ask
several questions.

7.1 Do Dynamic Approaches Answer a Broad Range of Phonological Questions?

The short answer to this question must be 'Yes'. Note the array of phenomena
that the DISC theory attempts to account for:

• precise timing of speech articulation
• common assimilatory processes
• vowel and consonant harmonies
• phonological representation
• syllabic and moraic structure

- stress and accentual phrases
- phonological typology
- phonological development
- physical and neural processes that realise all the above.

The space here does not allow us to critique whether DISC succeeds, but what started as an analysis of speech production implementation ends up looking a lot like a phonological theory. DISC may appear radical, restructuring much of phonological theory. There are no phonemes, only co-selection sets and activating fields. However, even if we put DISC to the side and focus on Turk and Shattuck-Hufnagel's (2020) XT/3C that preserved divisions between phonology and phonetics as well as syllables and phonemes, its phonology had several components not seen in classic structural phonology. The primary one was adding a section of the phonology that maps symbols towards qualitative and relational temporal and acoustic goals. We also used XT/3C as inspiration to posit a construction-like lexicon pairing phonemes with acoustic samples. This matching of a phonological goal to an auditory goal appeared within DISC as well, both in monitoring and in the possibility that acoustic samples are an input to intentional planning. The fact that both systems move in the direction of specifying goals in the phonological representation suggests that phonology needs target specification built into it, and we cannot separate articulatory grammatical patterns from acoustic grammatical patterns.[19] In short, every system we have reviewed that attempts to integrate dynamic aspects of language – aspects that must be integrated at some point in a full theory – eventuates a phonology quite different from phonologies without such integration.

7.2 Do These Dynamic Theories Advance Phonology?

The primary advancements from these approaches will be in the connections between phonology, speech production, and speech perception. Since duration and other timing matters must be considered in speech production and perception, theoretical development in those sub-fields can encroach on other sub-fields like phonology. Other advances are implicit in the theories themselves and do not need repeating here from earlier sections. One innovation I would like to highlight here is Harper's (2021) use of dynamic fields to control speech gestures to model variation.

One of the central questions of contemporary phonology is how to unite sociophonetic facts with phonological theories. The first requires large, patterned

---

[19] Arguably, this union exists in OT where constraints provide negative targets. However, both XT/3C and DISC include positive auditory targets. This is natural since both speech production models predict positive durations and forces.

variation while the latter can behave categorically (Bod, Hay, & Jannedy, 2003; Nagy, 2013). One way to address this is to enrich phonological representations. The idea that a word's phonology is a set of phonemes in an order (the place where this Element started) is put to the side. A general solution is to place significant variation into phonological representations themselves and then average over or abstract from that variation to allow for more categorical-like behaviour. One successful model that does this is exemplar theory (Pierrehumbert, 2001, 2003). An exemplar is an experience of each token of speech, such as words, syllables, or phones. Each of these exemplars is kept in memory, capturing all the variation the speaker encounters, along with social and distributive facts about those sounds. Exemplar theory then creates phonological representations that are incredibly rich to account for socio-phonetic facts, probabilistic patterns, and sub-phonemic variation (Foulkes & Doherty, 2006; Frisch, 2017; Guy, 2014). When a person speaks, they cannot utter this entire complexity at once. For that purpose, the exemplars are averaged over to create a target.

This work approaches phonology from the acoustic side (i.e., a rich representation is made of many different speech samples). Harper's (2021) work approaches from the production direction, offering a way for phonetic variation to have a dynamic *articulatory* basis. There are several sources of variation in the approach. First, the planning field has a preshape that is unique to the individual. This represents the most common way that an individual produces gestures of that type. Second, the distribution of the preshape can have broader and narrower variation. An individual with a broad preshape will show greater variation in articulation than one with a narrow preshape. This dispersion in preshape can also generate variation in how heard speech is categorised.

The third source of variation arises from the other components of the dynamic field equation, primarily the different sources of input. One input, as previously mentioned, is speech that has been heard. Over time, speakers would converge towards similar pronunciations. On the other hand, our speech production does not always match whatever is most frequent. Historical phonological change reveals cases where the most common variant of a sound does not always become the dominant one (Baxter et al., 2009). This also occurs where someone of a minority identity takes on speech patterns shared across a minority community different from the majority – even when they hear more speech from the majority.

A speaker does not model their speech simply based on frequency, but can weight some speech more than others in arriving at their own speech targets. Our neural oscillation work could give a mechanism for this that does not require adding a direct weighting mechanism to the system. The speech that we entrain with more fully, that which gets full attention, gets sampled more fully with a more detailed representation in the STG. One possibility then is that the speaker can direct attention to selected speech, even if it is not always the most frequent. By doing so, they build representations allowing the causal articulatory gesture to be recovered. This recovered heard gesture can then serve as a powerful input to modify the dynamic planning field.

Such an approach might be challenged by situations where speakers make their speech increasingly *dissimilar* to heard speech. In such cases, the location of the target on the dynamic planning field moves away from an input. We could consider that speakers simply are not paying attention to disfavoured speech and so it does not pull their speech towards it. This solution does not match situations where the speaker is aware of the disfavoured speech, however. Such speech or other stimuli has a negative effect on speaking choices (e.g., Drager, 2009; Hurring et al., 2022). Therefore, the same heard speech can send a dynamic planning field in two different directions based upon identity expression of the speaker before directly sending it as an input to planning.

7.3 What Is the Phonological Representation of the Lexicon?

The rich phonological representations of exemplar theory are not motivated solely by socio-phonetic facts. An additional motivation is how phonological patterns can vary through a lexicon. Put simply, some words in a language may exhibit a pattern absent from other words even when the words appear to have identical phonetic environments. If we store word-specific exemplars, however, then we might account for word-specific patterns (see also Bybee, 2003).

To address this in a DISC model, we need to consider what the lexicon might look like. The gestural score has the primary information required to utter the word. However, scores are not unitary things sitting in the brain. A gestural activation interval in a gestural score represents a duration where substantial energy exists to drive the musculature of the vocal tract. Gestural scores are dynamically assembled. The tract variable itself only has a specific meaning when the dynamic fields constituting its values are active. The score is a convenient representation of a process, a behaviour in time created in several interacting systems. We must retain something in long-term memory to represent the thousands of words we know, but scores are dynamically created ensembles, not file cards to retrieve and activate. An intentional planning field is simply a field capable of sustaining activation in a location on its surface. What makes its activation a value for a tract parameter is its connections to other areas, to the articulatory system, to a semantic system, to the speech perception system, and so on. These connections allow energy to flow from one area to the next. Therefore, we should expect the lexicon to reside in connections between areas, rather than individuated, localist representations sitting by thousands in the brain.

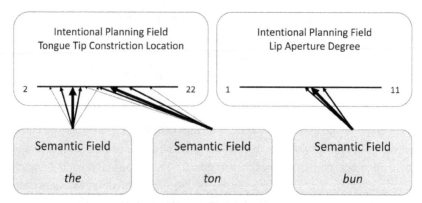

Figure 16 Semantic fields send excitation to intentional planning fields. The words *the* and *ton* will send excitation to the tongue tip intentional field, while *bun* will send excitation to the lip aperture field to drive the initial sounds. Moreover, *the* sends excitation more towards a dental place of articulation for the tongue tip, while *ton* sends excitation more towards an alveolar place. Relative levels of excitation are indicated by varying arrow size.

As a first approximation of a DISC-inspired lexicon, let us take the word *the*, the determiner. This will require choices of tongue tip, tongue body, and glottal gestures. The tongue tip should form a partial closure at the teeth, comprising the values for the tongue tip gesture. Other gestures will have their own values. When wishing to say *the*, the populations of neurons representing its meaning need to activate planning fields with the necessary values (Figure 16). We have not examined semantic representations, so we will just say a word has a semantic field, leaving what this means to future work. Rather than having the semantic field of *the* activate a phonological planning field of *the* (and the semantic field of *ton* activating the phonological planning field of *ton*, and the semantic field of *bun* activating the phonological planning field of *bun*), we need to imagine a network between the semantic fields and the intentional planning fields.

The strength of the connections between the semantic fields and the planning fields will vary. The field for *the* should maintain very strong connections to the dental value for the tongue tip, weaker connections to other tongue tips values like alveolar, and even weaker connections to unrelated gestures such as lip aperture. Conversely, *ton* would have strong connections to the alveolar value for the tongue tip and weaker connections to dental or lip aperture. *Bun* would connect strongly to a closure for lip aperture and weakly to tongue tip variables. In other words, the word is specified in the connections between semantics of words and the planning fields, not in maintaining thousands of different planning fields.

Therefore, we could store information about lexeme-specific phonological patterns by uniquely weighted connections from the semantic fields for those words to particular locations on the intentional planning fields. If one group of words has a higher /e/ than another group of words, this is kept as stronger connections to a higher tongue body gesture for one set of words than another set of words. We store exemplar-like information in the networks between areas. Similarly, experience with (beliefs about) different identities could manifest as stronger and weaker connections to different intentional planning areas. When an identity becomes active, it would send energy to one point on an intentional planning field different from another identity. The same process would occur with identification of individuals. We would expect that perceiving and producing words would be faster for identity matches than mismatches, because the identity sends additional activation along its path towards the intentional planning fields.

Storing the lexicon as a network between semantic and intentional planning fields cannot be the complete picture as it does not address serial order fully. Take the word *cat* /kɛt/. This would maintain strong connections between its semantic field and intentional planning fields for tongue body and tongue tip gestures. Recalling Tilsen (2016), we use competitive queuing to place the co-selection sets in the right order. The more active set will be produced first, so what is the activating agent to set these levels properly? One possibility is that the connections between semantic fields for words and intentional planning fields are stronger for co-selection sets that go earlier and weaker for those that go later. This results in higher activation for the early sets and so they are selected. This may work for well-known words where differing connections have been altered over longer periods of time, but how about words that we hear once and then produce? A possible solution here is to borrow the approach from the BUMP model of serial order: We use what we have heard as the activating agent context signal to guide production.

These solutions raise many questions we will not answer. The goal for us here is simply to indicate that work in dynamic field theory, such as that of Harper (2021), makes a significant contribution to this critical question about variability and abstraction in phonology, giving novel ideas for research and testing.

8 Conclusion

To conclude this work, I would like to ask again whether these dynamic approaches to phonological processing help us think differently about language than we might based purely on standard phonological structure.

One answer is, 'They have added to the discussion, but phonological grammars and phonological processing are really answers to two different questions.' This answer also might reference Marr's (1982) levels of analysis. Structural phonological grammars are at the computational level, wherein possibilities and impossibilities are calculated and expressed. The dynamic approaches here are, however, at the algorithmic level or even implementational. A computational grammar might be implemented in differing ways. From this perspective, the concepts are valuable for implementation but do not change the higher-level computational work, which is the normal domain of phonologists.

Rather than accepting this answer, I'd like to temporarily accept that these approaches do help us rethink phonology at a computational, not just implementational, level. To get at this, I would like to start in an unusual place, assessing the **problem of the homunculus**, first raised in discussion of slot-filler models. A homunculus is etymologically 'little person'. Imagine we want to give an account of a psychological process like visual perception. How does the brain know what we are looking at? One account might be that light enters our head through our eyes. The eyes themselves do not know what is being seen, so something else must. In the most literal version, a homunculus in our head knows what is being seen. But we wanted to explain how we know what we are seeing, and the homunculus answer does not help us because we have no idea how the homunculus knows anything. What is in the homunculus' head to handle visual perception? Maybe another homunculus. This is a potentially infinite regress. We keep positing more and more homunculi inside one another, none of which we actually understand.

Of course, theories of cognition do not frequently posit little people inside the brain. But homunculus-type arguments can still occur. If we want to know why a certain phonological pattern exists, we might set a rule providing the pattern. However, if the rule only expresses the pattern without a causal mechanism, then it requires another rule to explain it. This rule explaining the rule could require a rule as well. A homunculus trap emerges.

There might be an infinite regress in the DISC model that we have presented. Consider the intentional planning field, which sends activation towards articulation. That might explain the articulation, but why is the intentional planning field active? Perhaps a semantic field sent sufficient activation to the planning field. But why is the semantic field active? The regress starts to rear its head. Planning field excites planning field excites planning field.

The basics of neurons require this, however. Neurons never switch from a resting potential to an action potential – they never fire – sitting by themselves. They only spike when an electrochemical signal instigates the process.

In fact, dynamic neural fields do in fact go back indefinitely – and this is alright. The brain is never doing nothing. In a neuroimaging study of language, one cannot simply ask the participant to go in the fMRI, get them to do some language task, and then see where the languaging happens. The brain is constantly active, so you need a comparison point: one state where the participant is doing everything except the particular language process and one state where they are doing everything plus the language process. The difference provides an indication of where and when the language process is happening.

The key point here is simply that the brain never leaps to life from nothing. The current state is always connected to a previous state; the brain moves through its state space over time (i.e., it is a dynamic system). This is true all the way back to when neurons first develop in foetal development. If we accept that the mind is in fact a dynamic system, then we might wish to think of language that way as well (for different perspectives on this central idea, see Five Graces Group, 2009; Iskarous, 2016; Spivey, 2008). In this conception, language can be viewed as a set of energy flows and forces (Tilsen, 2019c). A dynamic intentional planning field gathers energy from other sources. When it possesses enough energy of its own in a coherent fashion, it sends energy towards articulation to force action.

If we revisit the forward models and monitoring, we see another reason to consider language as energy flows. During monitoring, the prediction error is calculated by comparing the speaker's prediction with the speaker's perception. But how do we actually calculate this? Recall that neural activation can be viewed as a probability distribution. The distance between the probability distribution representing the prediction and the distribution representing the perception comprises the prediction error. The distance between two distributions is a well-studied quantity called relative entropy (also the Kullback-Leibler Divergence; see Clark, 2013, 2015; Levy, 2008; Shannon, 1948).

Entropy is often called the amount of disorder in a system. Another way to think of it is how much information you would need to communicate the states of a system. If the entire system is a two-sided coin, then you can communicate its state by saying that it is heads or tails. This is one bit of information. A single neuron with a threshold can only fire or not fire, so it also contains one bit of information. If every neuron in a population of 1,000 neurons were to fire independently of each other, it would take 1,000 bits to specify its state. This is highly disorganised, takes lots of information to communicate, and has high entropy. However, if the neurons are firing in some pattern, then they are much more organised and would require less information to describe. At the limit, if all 1,000 neurons fired at the same time, the entire system reduces to one bit of information again: if you know what a single neuron is doing, then you know what the other 999 are doing. However, neurons would not all fire at the same time in a reliable way unless some other neurons are making them do so. A general result about entropy is that it increases over time. There are many more ways for neurons to all do their own thing than for them to follow a pattern. To reduce entropy – to sustain a pattern – energy must be used. In sum, language is a highly patterned activity with repeating, structured sounds, words, phrases, and so on. This implies that energy is constantly being utilised to create patterns. Any time that entropy reduces, we should look for a flow of energy (see also Friston, 2009, 2010).

The intention to say a word sends energy towards an intentional planning field. Planning fields send energy towards articulation. Energy is not only a metaphor here. Each neuron spends energy each time it fires. fMRI neuroimaging monitors oxygen flow to see what parts of the brain are using energy. Neural oscillations in speech perception can also be seen as energy flows. Without a coherent pattern, energy in the brain is diffuse and unable to drive another action. With an oscillatory pattern, however, that changes. A neuronal oscillation is a highly ordered state (Piai & Zheng, 2019), one that can be described with just a few parameters, such as period, phase, time, and amplitude. This is far more ordered than thousands of neurons firing randomly. Moving from a disordered state to an ordered one (or one with many degrees of freedom to few degrees of freedom) always requires energy. We must input energy to create this ordered state.

One of the central problems of contemporary phonological theory is how to integrate the highly varied data of socio-phonetics and usage-based phonetics with much less varied phonological patterns. We can now see that this is a point of entropy reduction, and so we can ask what energy flows make that possible. This perspective can also help us see neuronal oscillations differently. Our focus has been on oscillations as a sampling and serial order mechanism. However, an ordered oscillation of neural spiking is more able to drive action in another part of the brain than a disordered pattern. Oscillations concentrate energy into a wave that can push other areas such as semantic comprehension or speech production into action.

We saw these ideas of using energy to drive action and linguistic structure throughout the text.

- Exemplar models take many samples of speech and then reduce them to something narrower when comprehension or speech production occurs.
- Intentional planning fields take multiple inputs and create a single peak to initiate activation.

- Tilsen's motor sequencing field takes diverse input and generates an oscillating wave pattern that can boost activation in articulation.
- Our discussion of serial order mechanisms presented the context signal as a tool to select the right items at the right time. However, the context signal as well drives item selection, making them occur. Competitive queuing has an activation agent at its foundation.

Based on this, we can ask fascinating questions about language. Does a linguistic action reduce the number of possible states? If so, where does the energy come from? What are the flows of activation? What items are selected? Why and when? What connections exist to allow energy flow and how do those connections store, boost, or suppress future actions?

This all may sound very interesting, but talk of energy flows does not appear to answer questions linguists typically ask, such as what sounds exist in a language, where can they appear, how can they move, and so on.

This is partly a practical question. Certainly, there will be many tasks that linguists undertake that do not need a full analysis of energy flows, planning maps, and so on. The same is true, of course, for full phonological theory. There are many situations where transcribing IPA and making a few phonological rules to express a pattern is much more useful than extensive OT tableaux. Theory and practicality each have their place. At the same time, our dynamic approaches are making contributions towards questions phonologists commonly have. How many phonemes does a language have if a language has long vowels or consonants? The notion of selection and re-selection in DISC theory helps us answer this. Do all languages have the same phonological structure of phonemes, mora, and syllables? The idea of co-selection provides an answer for this. It also starts to give us a novel idea of what a constituent is. Constituents arise as pulses of energy, where their structure originates from the control processes selecting them.

This Element has moved from language as a hierarchical structure of things inside things, each with edges, to something new. Language in this new vision is a time course of energy waves that are coordinated through multiple people. There certainly is structure, but that structure is revealed by control processes: control of actions. What planning fields exist? What are their dynamics? How does information flow through time to different control fields? Many, many questions persist – excitingly. However, dynamic approaches do ask novel questions, provide a set of robust methodologies to investigate them, and can change the way we approach language structure itself.

References

Arvaniti, A. (2009). Rhythm, timing and the timing of rhythm. *Phonetica*, 66(1–2), 46–63.

Bauer, L., Warren, P., Bardsley, D., Kennedy, M., & Major, G. (2007). New Zealand English. *Journal of the International Phonetic Association*, 37(1), 97–102. http://doi.org/10.1017/S0025100306002830.

Baxter, G. J., Blythe, R. A., Croft, W., & McKane, A. J. (2009). Modeling language change: An evaluation of Trudgill's theory of the emergence of New Zealand English. *Language Variation and Change*, 21(2), 257–96. https://doi.org/10.1017/S095439450999010X.

Beckner, C., Blythe, R., Bybee, J., et al. (2009). Language is a complex adaptive system: Position paper. *Language Learning*, 59, 1–26. https://doi.org/10.1111/j.1467-9922.2009.00533.x.

Bod, R., Hay, J., & Jannedy, S. (2003). *Probabilistic Linguistics*. Cambridge, MA: MIT Press.

Boersma, P. (1998). *Functional Phonology: Formalizing the Interaction between Articulatory and Perceptual Drives*. The Hague: Holland Academic Graphics.

Bohland, J. W., Bullock, D., & Guenther, F. H. (2010). Neural representations and mechanisms for the performance of simple speech sequences. *Journal of Cognitive Neuroscience*, 22(7), 1504–29.

Boucher, V. J. (2021). *The Study of Speech Processes: Addressing the Writing Bias in Language Science*. Cambridge: Cambridge University Press.

Boucher, V. J., Gilbert, A. C., & Jemel, B. (2019). The role of low-frequency neural oscillations in speech processing: Revisiting delta entrainment. *Journal of Cognitive Neuroscience*, 31(8), 1–11. https://doi.org/10.1162/jocn_a_01410.

Bowers, J. S., Kazanina, N., & Andermane, N. (2016). Spoken word identification involves accessing position invariant phoneme representations. *Journal of Memory and Language*, 87, 71–83. https://doi.org/10.1016/j.jml.2015.11.002.

Browman, C. P., & Goldstein, L. M. (1986). Towards an articulatory phonology. *Phonology Yearbook*, 3, 219–52.

Browman, C. P., & Goldstein, L. M. (1989). Articulatory gestures as phonological units. *Phonology*, 6(2), 201–51.

Brown, G. D. A., Preece, T., & Hulme, C. (2000). Oscillator-based memory for serial order. *Psychological Review*, 107(1), 127–181. https://psycnet.apa.org/doi/10.1037/0033-295X.107.1.127.

Burgess, N., & Hitch, G. J. (1992). Towards a network model of the articulatory loop. *Journal of Memory and Language*, 31, 429–60.

Burgess, N., & Hitch, G. J. (1999). Memory for serial order: A network model of the phonological loop and its timing. *Psychological Review*, 106, 551–81.

Burgess, N., & Hitch, G. J. (2006). A revised model of short-term memory and long-term learning of verbal sequences. *Journal of Memory and Language*, 55, 627–52. https://doi.org/10.1016/j.jml.2006.08.005.

Buzsaki, G. (2006). *Rhythms of the Brain*. New York: Oxford University Press.

Bybee, J. (2003). *Phonology and Language Use* (vol. 94). Cambridge: Cambridge University Press.

Byrd, D. (1996). A phase window framework for articulatory timing. *Phonology*, 13, 139–69.

Clark, A. (2013). Whatever next? Predictive brains, situated agents, and the future of cognitive science. *Behavioral and Brain Sciences*, 36(3), 181–204. https://doi.org/10.1017/S0140525X12000477.

Clark, A. (2015). *Surfing Uncertainty: Prediction, Action, and the Embodied Mind*. Oxford: Oxford University Press.

Collins, J. (2019). Neural attractors and phonological grammar: What the sounds patterns of language can tell us about the brain (Doctoral thesis, The Arctic University of Norway).

Coltheart, M., & Rastle, K. (1994). Serial processing in reading aloud: Evidence for dual-route models of reading. *Journal of Experimental Psychology: Human Perception and Performance*, 20(6), 1197–211. https://doi.org/10.1037/0096-1523.20.6.1197.

Cutini, S., Szűcs, D., Mead, N., Huss, M., & Goswami, U. (2016). Atypical right hemisphere response to slow temporal modulations in children with developmental dyslexia. *Neuroimage*, 143, 40–9. https://doi.org/10.1016/j.neuroimage.2016.08.012.

De Saussure, F. (2011[1916]). *Course in General Linguistics*. New York: Columbia University Press.

Dell, G. S. (1986). A spreading activation theory of retrieval in sentence production. *Psychological Review*, 93, 283–321.

Di Lollo, V. (2012). The feature-binding problem is an ill-posed problem. *Trends in Cognitive Sciences*, 16(6), 317–21. https://doi.org/10.1016/j.tics.2012.04.007.

Donegan, P. J., & Stampe, D. (1979). The study of Natural Phonology. In D. Dinnsen, ed., *Current Approaches to Phonological Theory*. Bloomington: Indiana University Press, 126–73.

Drager, K. (2009). A sociophonetic ethnography of Selwyn Girls' High (Doctoral thesis, University of Canterbury).

Elliott, J. G. (2020). It's time to be scientific about dyslexia. *Reading Research Quarterly*, 55, S61–S75. https://doi.org/10.1002/rrq.333.

Erlhagen, W., & Schöner, G. (2002). Dynamic field theory of movement preparation. *Psychological Review*, 109(3), 545–72. https://doi.org/10.1037/0033-295x.109.3.545.

Evans, V. (2009). *How Words Mean: Lexical Concepts, Cognitive Models, and Meaning Construction*. Oxford: Oxford University Press.

Foulkes, P., & Docherty, G. (2006). The social life of phonetics and phonology. *Journal of Phonetics*, 34(4), 409–38. https://doi.org/10.1016/j.wocn.2005.08.002.

Fowler, C. A., Shankweiler, D., & Studdert-Kennedy, M. (2016). Perception of the speech code revisited: Speech is alphabetic after all. *Psychological Review*, 123(2), 125–50. https://doi.org/10.1037/rev0000013.

Fraga González, G., Karipidis, I. I., & Tijms, J. (2018). Dyslexia as a neurodevelopmental disorder and what makes it different from a chess disorder. *Brain Sciences*, 8(10), 189.

Frisch, S. A. (2017). Exemplar theories in phonology. In S. J. Hannahs & A. R. K. Bosch, eds., *The Routledge Handbook of Phonological Theory*. London: Routledge, 553–68.

Friston, K. (2009) The free-energy principle: A rough guide to the brain? *Trends in Cognitive Sciences*, 13(7), 293–301.

Friston, K. J. (2010) The free-energy principle: A unified brain theory? *Nature Reviews Neuroscience*, 11(2), 127–38.

Fusaroli, R., & Tylén, K. (2016). Investigating conversational dynamics: Interactive alignment, Interpersonal synergy, and collective task performance. *Cognitive Science*, 40(1), 145–71. https://doi.org/10.1111/cogs.12251.

Gafos, A., & Kirov, C. (2009). A dynamical model of change in phonological representations: The case of lenition. In J. Chitoran, E. Marsico, F. Pellegrino, & C. Coupé, eds., *Approaches to Phonological Complexity*. Berlin: Mouton de Gruyter, 219–40.

Galantucci, B., Fowler, C. A., & Turvey, M. T. (2006). The motor theory of speech perception reviewed. *Psychonomic Bulletin & Review*, 13(3), 361–77.

Ghitza, O. (2011). Linking speech perception and neurophysiology: Speech decoding guided by cascaded oscillators locked to the input rhythm. *Frontiers in Psychology*, 2, 1–13. https://doi: 10.3389/fpsyg.2011.00130.

Ghitza, O., & Greenberg, S. (2009). On the possible role of brain rhythms in speech perception: Intelligibility of time-compressed speech with periodic and aperiodic insertions of silence. *Phonetica*, 66, 113–26. https://doi.org/10.1159/000208934.

Giraud, A.-L., & Poeppel, D. (2012). Cortical oscillations and speech processing: Emerging computational principles and operations. *Nature Neuroscience*, 15(4), 511–17. https://doi.org/10.1038/nn.3063.

Goldberg, A. E. (2006). *Constructions at Work: The Nature of Generalization in Language*. Oxford: Oxford University Press.

Goldberg, A., & Suttle, L. (2010). Construction grammar. *Wiley Interdisciplinary Reviews: Cognitive Science*, 1(4), 468–77.

Goldstein, L., & Iskarous, K. (2018). The dynamics of prominence profiles: From local computation to global patterns. In D. Brentari & J. L. Lee, eds., *Shaping Phonology*. Chicago: University of Chicago Press, 253–77.

Goldstein, L., Nam, H., Saltzman, E., & Chitoran, I. (2009). Coupled oscillator planning model of speech timing and syllable structure. In C. Fant, M. Gunnar, H. Fujisaki, & J. Shen, eds., *Frontiers in Phonetics and Speech Science*. Shanghai: The Commercial Press, 239–49.

Goswami, U. (2011). A temporal sampling framework for developmental dyslexia. *Trends in Cognitive Sciences*, 15(1), 3–10. https://doi.org/10.1016/j.tics.2010.10.001.

Grabe, E., & Low, E. L. (2002) Durational variability in speech and the rhythm class hypothesis. In C. Gussenhoven & N. Warner, eds., *Laboratory Phonology 7*. Berlin: Mouton deGruyter, 515–46.

Grossberg, S. (1978). A theory of human memory: Self-organization and performance of sensory-motor codes, maps, and plans. In R. Rosen & F. Snell, eds., *Progress in Theoretical Biology*. New York: Academic Press, 233–374.

Guenther, F. H. (2016). *Neural Control of Speech*. Cambridge, MA: MIT Press

Guy, G. R. (2014). Linking usage and grammar: Generative phonology, exemplar theory, and variable rules. *Lingua*, 142, 57–65. https://doi.org/10.1016/j.lingua.2012.07.007.

Haegens, S., & Golumbic, E. Z. (2018). Rhythmic facilitation of sensory processing: A critical review. *Neuroscience & Biobehavioral Reviews*, 86, 150–65. https://doi.org/10.1016/j.neubiorev.2017.12.002.

Hämäläinen, J. A., Rupp, A., Soltész, F., Szücs, D., & Goswami, U. (2012). Reduced phase locking to slow amplitude modulation in adults with dyslexia: An MEG study. *Neuroimage*, 59(3), 2952–61. https://doi.org/10.1016/j.neuroimage.2011.09.075.

Harper, S. (2021). Individual differences in phonetic variability and phonological representation (Doctoral thesis, University of Southern California).

Hartley, T., Hurlstone, M. J., & Hitch, G. J. (2016). Effects of rhythm on memory for spoken sequences: A model and tests of its stimulus-driven mechanism. *Cognitive Psychology*, 87, 135–78. http://dx.doi.org/10.1016/j.cogpsych.2016.05.001.

Hayes, B. (1995). *Metrical Stress Theory: Principles and Case Studies*. Chicago: University of Chicago Press.

Hitch, G. J., Hurlstone, M. J., & Hartley, T. (2022). Computational models of working memory for language. In J. W. Schwieter & W. Zhisheng, eds., *The Cambridge Handbook of Working Memory and Language*. Cambridge: Cambridge University Press, 143–74.

Hoffmann, T., & Trousdale, G. (2013). *The Oxford Handbook of Construction Grammar*. Oxford: Oxford University Press.

Houghton, G., & Hartley, T. (1995). Parallel models of serial behavior: Lashley revisited. *Psyche*, 2(25), 1–25.

Hurlstone, M. J. (2021). Serial recall. In M. J. Kahana, & A. D. Wagner, eds., *The Oxford Handbook of Human Memory*. Oxford: Oxford University Press.

Hurring, G., Hay, J., Drager, K., Podlubny, R., Manhire, L., & Ellis, A. (2022). Social priming in speech perception: Revisiting kangaroo/kiwi priming in New Zealand English. *Brain Sciences*, 12(6), 684. https://doi.org/10.3390/brainsci12060684.

Iskarous, K. (2016). Compatible dynamical models of environment, sensory, and perceptual systems. *Ecological Psychology*, 28(4), 295–311. http://dx.doi.org/10.1080/10407413.2016.1230377.

Izhikevich, E. M (2010). *Dynamical Systems in Neuroscience: The Geometry of Excitability and Bursting*. Cambridge, MA: MIT Press.

Jones, M. R. (1976). Time, our lost dimension: Toward a new theory of perception, attention, and memory. *Psychological Review*, 83, 323–35.

Jones, M. R. (1986). Attentional rhythmicity in human perception. In J. R. Evans & M. Clynes, eds., *Rhythm in Psychological, Linguistic and Musical Processes*. Springfield, IL: Charles C Thomas, Publisher, 13–40.

Jun, S. A. (Ed.). (2005). *Prosodic Typology: The Phonology of Intonation and Phrasing*. Oxford: Oxford University Press.

Kandel, E. R., Schwartz, J. H., Jessell, T. M., Siegelbaum, S., Hudspeth, A. J., & Mack, S., eds. (2000). *Principles of Neural Science*. New York: McGraw-Hill.

Kazanina, N., Bowers, J. S., & Idsardi, W. (2018). Phonemes: Lexical access and beyond. *Psychonomic Bulletin & Review*, 25(2), 560–85. https://doi.org/10.3758/s13423-017-1362-0.

Kemmerer, D. (2014). *Cognitive Neuroscience of Language*. London: Psychology Press.

Kirchner, R. M. (1998). *An Effort-Based Approach to Consonant Lenition* (Doctoral thesis, University of California, Los Angeles).

Lakatos, P., Musacchia G., O'Connell, M. N., et al. (2013) The spectrotemporal filter mechanism of auditory selective attention. *Neuron*, 77, 750–61. https://doi.org/10.1016/j.neuron.2012.11.034.

Large, E. W., & Jones, M. R. (1999). The dynamics of attending: How people track time-varying events. *Psychological Review*, 106(1), 119–59. https://doi .org/10.1037/0033-295X.106.1.119.

Lashley, K. S. (1951). *The Problem of Serial Order in Behavior*. Oxford: Bobbs-Merrill.

Lehiste, I. (1977). Isochrony reconsidered. *Journal of Phonetics*, 5(3), 253–63.

Levelt, W. J. (1993). *Speaking: From Intention to Articulation*. Cambridge, MA: MIT press.

Levy, R. (2008). Expectation-based syntactic comprehension. *Cognition*, 106(3), 1126–77.

Lewandowsky, S., & Farrell, S. (2008). Short-term memory: New data and a model. *The Psychology of Learning and Motivation*, 49, 1–48. https://doi .org/10.1016/S0079-7421(08)00001-7.

Liang, P., Wu, S., & Gu, F. (2016). *An Introduction to Neural Information Processing*. Dordrecht: Springer.

Liberman, A. M., & Mattingly, I. G. (1985). The motor theory of speech perception revised. *Cognition*, 21(1), 1–36.

Lisman, J. E., & Jensen, O. (2013) The theta-gamma neural code. *Neuron*, 77, 1002–16. https://doi.org/10.1016/j.neuron.2013.03.007.

Lizarazu, M., Lallier, M., Molinaro, N., Bourguignon, M., et al. (2015). Developmental evaluation of atypical auditory sampling in dyslexia: Functional and structural evidence. *Human Brain Mapping*, 36(12), 4986–5002. https://doi.org/10.1002/hbm.22986.

Logan, G. D. (2018). Automatic control: How experts act without thinking. *Psychological Review*, 125(4), 453-85.

Luo, H., & Poeppel, D. (2007). Phase patterns of neuronal responses reliably discriminate speech in human auditory cortex. *Neuron*, 54, 1001–10. https:// doi.org/10.1016/j.neuron.2007.06.004.

Marr, D. (1982). *Vision: A Computational Approach*. San Francisco: Freeman & Co.

McClelland, J. L., & Elman, J. L. (1986). The TRACE model of speech perception. *Cognitive Psychology*, 18(1), 1–86.

Mesgarani, N., & Chang, E.F. (2012) Selective cortical representation of attended speaker in multi-talker speech perception. *Nature*, 485, 233–6. https://doi.org/10.1038/nature11020.

Meyer, L. (2018) The neural oscillations of speech processing and language comprehension: State of the art and emerging mechanisms. *European Journal of Neuroscience*, 28, 2609–2621. https://doi.org/ 10.1111/ejn.13748.

Miller, G. A. (1956). The magical number seven, plus or minus two: Some limits on our capacity for processing information. *Psychological Review*, 63(2), 81–97. https://doi.org/10.1037/h0043158.

Mills, G. J. (2014). Dialogue in joint activity: Complementarity, convergence and conventionalization. *New Ideas in Psychology*, 32, 158–73. https://doi.org/10.1016/j.newideapsych.2013.03.006.

Monahan, P. J., Schertz, J., Fu, Z., & Pérez, A. (2022). Unified coding of spectral and temporal phonetic cues: Electrophysiological evidence for abstract phonological features. *Journal of Cognitive Neuroscience*, 34(4), 618–38. https://doi.org/10.1162/jocn_a_01817.

Munson, B., McDonald, E. C., DeBoe, N. L., & White, A. R. (2006). The acoustic and perceptual bases of judgments of women and men's sexual orientation from read speech. *Journal of Phonetics*, 34(2), 202–40.

Nagy, N. (2013). Phonology and sociolinguistics. In R. Bayley, R. Cameron, and C. Lucas, eds., *The Oxford Handbook of Sociolinguistics*. Oxford: Oxford University Press, pp. 425-444.

Nathan, G. S. (2008). *Phonology: A Cognitive Grammar Introduction*. Amsterdam: John Benjamins

Oganian, Y., & Chang, E. F. (2019). A speech envelope landmark for syllable encoding in human superior temporal gyrus. *Science Advances*, 5(11), 1–13. https://doi.org/10.1126/sciadv.aay6279.

Oganian, Y., Fox, N. P., & Chang, E. F. (2022). Cortical representation of speech sounds: Insights from intracranial electrophysiology of speech sound processing. In L.L. Holt, J. E. Peelle, A. B. Coffin, A. N. Popper, & R. R. Fay, eds., *Speech Perception*. New York: The ASA Press, 45–80.

Ojemann, G. A. (1987). Surgical therapy for medically intractable epilepsy. *Journal of Neurosurgery*, 66(4), 489–99. https://doi.org/10.3171/jns.1987.66.4.0489.

Ostrand, R., & Chodroff, E. (2021). It's alignment all the way down, but not all the way up: Speakers align on some features but not others within a dialogue. *Journal of Phonetics*, 88, article 101074. https://doi.org/10.1016/j.wocn.2021.101074.

O'Sullivan, J. A., Herrero, J., Smith, E. et al. (2019). Hierarchical encoding of attended auditory objects in multi-talker speech perception. *Neuron*, 104(6), 1195–209. https://doi.org/10.1016/j.neuron.2019.09.007.

Pasley, B. N., David, S. V., Mesgarani, N., et al. (2012). Reconstructing speech from human auditory cortex. *PLoS Biology*, 10(1), article e1001251. https://doi.org/10.1371/journal.pbio.1001251.

Peelle, J. E. & Davis, M. H. (2012) Neural oscillations carry speech rhythm through to comprehension. *Frontiers in Psychology*, 3, article 320. https://doi.org/10.3389/fpsyg.2012.00320.

Piai, V., & Zheng, X. (2019). Chapter Eight – Speaking waves: Neuronal oscillations in language production. *Psychology of Learning and Motivation*, 71, 265–302. https://doi.org/10.1016/bs.plm.2019.07.002.

Pickering, M. J., & Clark, A. (2014). Getting ahead: Forward models and their place in cognitive architecture. *Trends in Cognitive Science*, 18(9), 451–56. http://dx.doi.org/10.1016/j.tics.2014.05.006.

Pickering, M. J., & Garrod, S. (2004). Toward a mechanistic psychology of dialogue. *Behavioral and Brain Sciences*, 27(2), 169–90. https://doi.org/10.1017/S0140525X04000056.

Pickering, M. J., & Garrod, S. (2013). An integrated theory of language production and comprehension. *Behavioral and Brain Sciences*, 36(4), 329–47. https://doi.org/10.1017/S0140525X12001495.

Pickering, M. J., & Garrod, S. (2014). Self-, other-, and joint monitoring using forward models. *Frontiers in Human Neuroscience*, 8, article 132. https://doi.org/10.3389/fnhum.2014.00132.

Pierrehumbert, J. (2001). Exemplar dynamics: Word frequency, lenition, and contrast. In J. Bybee and P. Hopper, eds., *Frequency Effects and the Emergence of Linguistic Structure*. Amsterdam: John Benjamins, Amsterdam, 137–57.

Pierrehumbert, J. B. (2003) Phonetic diversity, statistical learning, and acquisition of phonology. *Language and Speech*, 46, 115–54.

Protopas, A. (2014). From temporal processing to developmental language disorders: mind the gap. Philosophical Transactions of the Royal Society B, 369, 1–11. https://doi.org/10.1098/rstb.2013.0090.

Protopapas, A., & Parrila, R. (2018). Is dyslexia a brain disorder? *Brain Sciences*, 8(4), 61. http://doi.org/10.3390/brainsci8040061.

Ramus, F., Nespor, M., & Mehler, J. (1999). Correlates of linguistic rhythm in the speech signal. *Cognition*, 73, 265–92.

Roelofs, A. (1997). The WEAVER model of word-form encoding in speech production. *Cognition*, 64, 249–84.

Roon, K. D., & Gafos, A. I. (2016). Perceiving while producing: Modeling the dynamics of phonological planning. *Journal of Memory and Language*, 89, 222–43. https://doi.org/10.1016/j.jml.2016.01.005.

Saltzman, E., & Byrd, D. 2000. Task-dynamics of gestural timing: Phase windows and multifrequency rhythms. *Human Movement Science*, 19, 499–526.

Saltzman, E. L., & Munhall, K. G. 1989. A dynamical approach to gestural patterning in speech production. *Ecological Psychology*, 1, 333–82

Saltzman, E., Nam, H., Krivokapic, J., & Goldstein, L. (2008). A task-dynamic toolkit for modeling the effects of prosodic structure on articulation.

In P. A. Barbosa, S. Madureira, & C. Reis, eds., *Proceedings of the Speech Prosody 2008 Conference*. Campinas: Editora RG/CNPq.

Samuel, A. G. (2020). Psycholinguists should resist the allure of linguistic units as perceptual units. *Journal of Memory and Language*, 111, 1–12. https://doi .org/10.1016/j.jml.2019.104070.

Sasisekaran, J. (2012). Effects of delayed auditory feedback on speech kinematics in fluent speakers. *Perceptual and Motor Skills*, 115(3), 845–64. https://doi.org/10.2466/15.22.PMS.115.6.845-864.

Schöner, G., & Spencer, J. (2015). *Dynamic Thinking: A Primer on Dynamic Field Theory*. Oxford: Oxford University Press.

Sedivy, J. (2019). *Language in Mind: An Introduction to Psycholinguistics* (2nd ed.). Oxford: Oxford University Press.

Segalowitz, S. J., & Chevalier, H. (1998). Event-related potential (ERP) research in neurolinguistics, part I, techniques and applications to lexical access. In B. E. Stemmer & H. A. Whitaker, eds., *Handbook of Neurolinguistics*. San Diego: Academic Press, 95–109.

Shattuck-Hufnagel, S. (1979). Speech errors as evidence for a serial-ordering mechanism in sentence production. In W. E. Cooper & E. C. T. Walker, eds., *Sentence Processing: Psycholinguistic Studies Presented to Merrill Garrett*. Hillsdale, NJ: Erlbaum, 295–342.

Shannon, C. E. (1948). A mathematical theory of communication. *The Bell System Technical Journal*, 27(3), 379–423.

Spivey, M. (2008). *The Continuity of Mind*. Oxford: Oxford University Press.

Spivey, M., Joanisse, M., & McRae, K. (Eds.). (2012). *The Cambridge Handbook of Psycholinguistics*. Cambridge: Cambridge University Press.

Stevens, K. N. (2002). Toward a model for lexical access based on acoustic landmarks and distinctive features. *The Journal of the Acoustical Society of America*, 111(4), 1872–91.

Stevens, K. N., & Halle, M. (1967) Remarks on the analysis by synthesis and distinctive features. In W. Walthen-Dunn, ed., *Models for the Perception of Speech and Visual Form*. Cambridge, MA: MIT Press, 88–102.

St. Pierre, T., Cooper, A., & Johnson, E. K. (2021). Cross-generational phonetic alignment between mothers and their children. *Language Learning and Development*, 18(4), 393–414. https://doi.org/10.1080/15475441.2021 .1979401.

Tilsen, S. (2013). A dynamical model of hierarchical selection and coordination in speech planning. *PLoS One*, 8(4), article e62800. https://doi.org/10.1371/ journal.pone.0062800.

Tilsen, S. (2014). Selection-coordination theory. Cornell Working Papers in Phonetics and Phonology.

Tilsen, S. (2016). Selection and coordination: The articulatory basis for the emergence of phonological structure. *Journal of Phonetics*, 55, 53–77. https://doi.org/10.1016/j.wocn.2015.11.005.

Tilsen, S. (2018). Three mechanisms for modeling articulation: Selection, coordination, and intention. Cornell Working Papers in Phonetics and Phonology.

Tilsen, S. (2019a). Motoric mechanisms for the emergence of non-local phono-logical patterns. *Frontiers in Psychology*, 10, 2143. https://doi.org/10.3389/fpsyg.2019.02143.

Tilsen, S. (2019b). Space and time in models of speech rhythm. *Annals of the New York Academy of Sciences*, 1453(1), 47–66. https://doi.org/10.1111/nyas.14102.

Tilsen, S. (2019c). *Syntax with Oscillators and Energy Levels*. Berlin: Language Science Press.

Tilsen, S. (2020). Detecting anticipatory information in speech with signal chopping. *Journal of Phonetics*, 82, 1–26. https://doi.org/10.1016/j.wocn.2020.100996.

Tune, S., & Obleser, J. (2022). A parsimonious look at neural oscillations in speech perception. In L. L. Holt, J. E. Peelle, A. B. Coffin, A. N. Popper, & R. R. Fay, eds., *Speech Perception*. New York: The ASA Press, 81–112.

Turk, A., & Shattuck-Hufnagel, S. (2013). What is speech rhythm? A commentary inspired by Arvaniti & Rodriquez, Krivokapić, and Goswami & Leong. *Laboratory Phonology*, 4(1), 93–118.

Turk, A., & Shattuck-Hufnagel, S. (2020). *Speech Timing: Implications for Theories of Phonology, Phonetics, and Speech Motor Control*. Oxford: Oxford University Press.

van Geert, P. (1991). A dynamic systems model of cognitive and language growth. *Psychological Review*, 98(1), 3–53. https://doi.org/10.1037/0033-295X.98.1.3.

van Geert, P. (2003). Dynamic systems approaches and modeling of developmental processes. In Schinka, J. A., Velicer, W. F., Healy, A. F., et al., eds., *Handbook of Developmental Psychology*. New York: Sage Publications,640–72.

Vousden, J. I., Brown, G. D., & Harley, T. A. (2000). Serial control of phon-ology in speech production: A hierarchical model. *Cognitive Psychology*, 41(2), 101–75.

White, L., & Mattys, S. L. (2007). Calibrating rhythm: First language and second language studies. *Journal of Phonetics*, 35, 501–22. https://doi.org/10.1016/j.wocn.2007.02.003.

Wijnants, M. L., Hasselman, F., Cox, R. F. A., Bosman, A. M. T., & Van Orden, G. (2012). An interaction-dominant perspective on reading fluency and dyslexia. *Annals of Dyslexia*, 62(2), 100–19. https://doi.org/10.1007/s11881-012-0067-3.

Wolpert, D.M. (1997). Computational approaches to motor control. *Trends in Cognitive Science*, 1, 209–16. https://doi.org/10.1016/s1364-6613(97)01070-x.

Cambridge Elements $\equiv$

Psycholinguistics

Paul Warren
Victoria University of Wellington

Paul Warren is Professor of Linguistics at Victoria University of Wellington, where his teaching and research is in psycholinguistics, phonetics, and laboratory phonology. His publications include *Introducing Psycholinguistics* (2012) and *Uptalk* (2016), both published by CUP. He is a founding member of the Association for Laboratory Phonology, and a member of the Australasian Speech Science Technology Association and the International Phonetic Association. Paul is a member of the editorial boards for *Laboratory Phonology* and the *Journal of the International Phonetic Association*, and for twenty years (2000–2019) served on the editorial board of *Language and Speech*.

Advisory Board

About the Series

This Elements series presents theoretical and empirical studies in the interdisciplinary field of psycholinguistics. Topics include issues in the mental representation and processing of language in production and comprehension, and the relationship of psycholinguistics to other fields of research. Each Element is a high quality and up-to-date scholarly work in a compact, accessible format.

Cambridge Elements ☰

Psycholinguistics

Elements in the Series

Verbal Irony Processing
Stephen Skalicky

Grammatical Encoding for Speech Production
Linda Ruth Wheeldon and Agnieszka Konopka

Dynamic Approaches to Phonological Processing
Hunter Hatfield

A full series listing is available at: www.cambridge.org/EPSL

Printed in the USA
CPSIA information can be obtained
at www.ICGtesting.com
LVHW011302150324
774517LV00048B/2569